The Simple Guide to Complex Trauma and Dissociation

The Simple Guide to Complex Trauma and Dissociation

What It Is and How to Help

Betsy de Thierry

Foreword by Graham Music

Illustrated by Emma Reeves

Jessica Kingsley Publishers
London and Philadelphia

First published in Great Britain in 2021 by Jessica Kingsley Publishers
An Hachette Company

5

A CIP catalogue record for this title is available from the British Library and the
Library of Congress

ISBN 978 1 78775 314 3
eISBN 978 1 78775 315 0

Printed and bound in Great Britain by Clays Ltd.

Jessica Kingsley Publishers' policy is to use papers that are natural, renewable and
recyclable products and made from wood grown in sustainable forests. The logging and
manufacturing processes are expected to conform to the environmental regulations of
the country of origin.

Jessica Kingsley Publishers
73 Collier Street
London N1 9BE, UK

www.jkp.com

CONTENTS

FOREWORD

It is a huge privilege to introduce this wonderful new book, the latest in a series in which Betsy de Thierry takes complicated and hard to digest topics – ones which urgently need to be understood and disseminated to wider populations – and somehow manages to make challenging ideas both comprehensible and useable.

Trauma, and complex trauma especially, is hard to think about for a number of reasons. Almost by definition, trauma is unmanageable and unthinkable, affecting not only the traumatised person, but also those in their orbit, which includes professionals. This vicarious trauma is a deadly serious issue, often leading to burnout and post-traumatic stress disorder (PTSD) symptoms.

Trauma comes in various flavours and each needs a separate approach, something it has taken many of us too many years of unhelpful practice, of failing too many clients, to learn. de Thierry puts us straight on much of this. For much of my career it was not recognised that talking to someone about their trauma can be re-triggering rather than helpful and can lead to the re-emergence of trauma symptoms. In the early days we certainly knew very little about dissociation and states such as derealisation or depersonalisation, let alone what is now called Dissociative Identity Disorder, which was barely recognised. We now know that such symptoms are central in many serious trauma cases, but still easily missed. de Thierry takes us firmly and gently by the hand to walk us through this complex and often frightening labyrinth, and in reading this book the reader will breathe a sigh of relief, as the terrifying maze is transformed into a clearer path.

A tragedy of developmental trauma is that the roots of the personality are so deeply affected, and de Thierry spells out many of the ways in which this happens. Too many children and young people suffering trauma do not receive the help and understanding they need in order to heal, or re-grow hope and confidence that life can offer them what they need. Too many get cast into inappropriate boxes or categories, such as attention deficit hyperactivity disorder (ADHD) or autism spectrum disorder (ASD), or as 'bad' and 'criminal'. What then gets lost is the human being who is suffering and who needs reaching out to, who will recover only from ongoing relationships where they feel understood and cared for, in which they can develop faith in their ability to grow, to love and be loved, and through that begin to heal from trauma.

This is made worse because so many children who are victims of trauma can seem hard to like, can seem unfriendly, untrusting and do not evoke the desire to help in the very people they need help from. Many from traumatised backgrounds struggle, for example, to manage basic interpersonal reciprocity and do not understand how relationships work. Too often, having missed out on the building blocks of cooperation or mutual care, they lack the capacity to even recognise, let alone receive, good care from benign others.

Over decades I have consistently seen abused, traumatised or neglected children punished for traits which they develop to survive in their early lives. Hypervigilance, jumpiness or reactivity were often what they needed in their original homes but are a handicap in schools or adoptive families. So many struggle with anything they cannot control – the novel, uncertainty, perhaps a shift in school routine, such as a temporary teacher. Such seemingly small events can trigger chaotic, acting-out or withdrawn behaviours, all signs of extremely anxious feelings just below the surface, of a fundamental lack of faith in life, of little belief that new experiences are likely to turn out well.

We learn basic relational patterns early in life, such as how sensible it is to relax, or alternatively, to brace for trouble, or shut down in numb dissociation. We similarly learn, often preverbally, whether it is a good idea to be dependent or self-reliant, hopeful or fearful, trusting or suspicious, tense or easeful. Children who suffer trauma are far less likely to expect good outcomes or believe it is safe to depend on others or allow vulnerability, often seeing danger when others see safety.

Freud long ago described the pleasure principle, the simple idea that humans, like most species, move towards pleasure and away from pain. For too many troubled kids, relationships and intimacy signal danger rather than pleasure. Such expectations of relationships, our 'internal working models' (Bowlby 1969), influence how our minds and bodies respond to new circumstances.

When we feel safe the 'rest and digest' part of our nervous system comes online. This increases the likelihood of trust and close relationships. This also has positive physical benefits, including lower heart-rate and blood pressure, deeper breathing and better digestive and immune systems. Yet when life feels scary and dangerous, such positive emotional systems are turned off. de Thierry provides an easy-to-follow map which helps us navigate these complex issues.

Effective help for trauma requires the fundamental understandings that this book provides so subtly yet profoundly. It requires an understanding of when people need help to become more embodied, how to recognise and work with dissociative states, when to face traumatic memories and when to build safeness and good internal resources instead. We need to know when it is helpful to try to tune down reactive fear states, and how we can facilitate feelings of safety, and openness to others.

For good reasons, therapeutic trainings encourage processing of difficult and frightening experiences, painful emotions, aggressive or despairing parts of the personality. New understandings of trauma, such as we read about here, explain why it is vital to also build positive, safety-based feeling states. Putting people in touch with the trauma too quickly can be like prodding an open wound with a sharp instrument. It can trigger re-traumatisation, redoubling defences and, more worryingly, dissociative states, including flashbacks, and feeling as if terrifying past events are happening in the present. de Thierry shows us how we can help grow and develop parts of the personality capable of providing a sense of safety, calm and trust, which all need to be built before facing trauma head-on. It is only from such a secure vantage point that we can safely manage to revisit and process traumatic experiences.

de Thierry captures all this admirably, not shirking the complex or frightening nature of traumatic experiences, but always making them understandable, bearable, and giving us the courage to know that they are workable with, that pain can be faced, that growth is always possible and what tools can help; and for this therapists and a range of professionals, parents and carers will be very grateful.

Graham Music, PhD,
consultant child psychotherapist at the Tavistock Centre, adult
psychotherapist in private practice and author of Nurturing Children:
From Trauma to Hope Using Neurobiology, Psychoanalysis
and Attachment *(2019),* Nurturing Natures *(2016),* Affect
and Emotion *(2001) and* The Good Life *(2014)*

INTRODUCTION

This book has been written to enable professionals who work with children and young people to understand the complex subject of recovery from complex trauma.

It will also help support parents and carers involved in caring for those children and young people who have experienced complex trauma.

You will get the most out of this book if you read it as a complement to another book in this series, *The Simple Guide to Child Trauma*, which explores the impact of trauma, how to help a child recover and how resilience can be built. (That is not to try and sell other books, but my aim has been to write short books that cover different complex issues in a brief, readable way – it falls beyond the scope of a single simple guide to cover the foundations of general trauma recovery too.) So, as stated in the title, this book has a particular focus on complex trauma.

Trauma can be defined as an event that causes the person to feel terrified, powerless and overwhelmed. Trauma can impact a child's body, brain, memory, emotions, relationships, learning and behaviour.

The traumatic experience and the impact of it can vary in severity, which is discussed in the book. Type I trauma is a single incident trauma, Type II is prolonged trauma and

Type III is trauma that is repeated, prolonged and can include being hurt by those who were meant to take care of you. This book is all about Type III trauma and the impact of it and recovery from it.

The National Child Traumatic Stress Network describes complex trauma like this:

> Complex trauma describes both children's exposure to multiple traumatic events – often of an invasive, inter-personal nature – and the wide-ranging, long-term effects of this exposure. These events are severe and pervasive, such as abuse or profound neglect. They usually occur early in life and can disrupt many aspects of the child's development and the formation of a sense of self. Since these events often occur with a caregiver, they interfere with the child's ability to form a secure attachment. (NCTSN n.d.)

At present, many children who have experienced trauma seem to end up with many different medical diagnoses, such as attention deficit hyperactivity disorder (ADHD), oppositional defiance disorder (ODD), etc; based on my experience with hundreds of families, those making the diagnoses don't take into account the history of trauma but rather offer labels that indicate ill-health that appeared out of nowhere or is genetic.

Very often within the mental health system, there seems to be little talk of the correlation between what happened to the child and how they are now responding and therefore there seems to be little knowledge and skill available to enable these children to recover from all the trauma symptoms that are hindering their life.

I fully believe that recovery is possible and I have files and files of clinical measures that show the journey from significant, life-altering trauma symptoms to a life that is much like anyone else's. I have seen it in the organisations I lead and many of the books in my references explore stories of children and young people who have recovered from significant complex trauma (*see* Silberg 2013; Waters 2016; Wieland 2011).

I don't believe that focusing solely on diagnosis and medication leads to a healing approach, and this book offers a recovery framework as an alternative.

This book is written from the premise that – when a person has had moments in their life where they thought they were not going to be able to survive, either from feeling alone and abandoned due to lack of help when they were in a state of overwhelm, or when they were hurt by others – this is trauma and they will now most probably have internal or external symptoms as a result.

Adverse childhood experiences (ACEs) is a concept that more people are aware of. The difference between adversity and trauma is that adversity describes the experience and trauma describes the short-term and longer-term impact of that experience.

I believe we need to teach our children and young people that the majority of symptoms of trauma are exactly that – symptoms, coping mechanisms and defensive systems formed because of what they experienced. It is no different to someone having a broken leg due to falling off a bike who needs to do a few things to help his leg heal; these children gave been hurt psychologically and now need appropriate treatment to help them heal. There are a lot of young people scared that there is something wrong with them and many currently have no hope of recovery right now because they need to understand the impact of trauma. Of course there could be what is called 'comorbidity', which describes when the child has got some other medical challenge, such as fetal alcohol syndrome, epilepsy, autism or other health and wellbeing issues. We can't assume that everything is trauma, but we can certainly always look with 'trauma glasses' to see what we can do that can help resolve the trauma symptoms so that we can see what symptoms are left.

Of course, studying the science of the invisible is complex! There are constant changing thoughts, research and ideas as we understand more of our invisible subconscious and psyche. There are mountains of incredible writing about this subject; this book is designed as a 'simple guide' to the subject to help people get an overview and introduction to a complex subject.

Some children who experience distress having experienced trauma are given a diagnosis of post-traumatic stress disorder (PTSD). That can lead to many of them having other diagnoses that do not seem to recognise the trauma history and so are not recovery-focused. Sadly, when a child has a diagnosis of 'behavioural problems' or ADHD or ODD, it can sometimes hold the child back from achieving their full potential because of the long-term label. Dr Bessel van der Kolk and his colleagues within the National Child Traumatic Stress Network in 2009 suggested the term 'developmental trauma', to encapsulate the impact of multiple childhood traumas. They were hoping it could be put into the *Diagnostic and Statistical Manual of Mental Disorders*,

Fifth edition (*DSM-5*; APA 2013). The criteria included the following: exposure to trauma, affective and physiological dysregulation, attentional and behavioural dysregulation, self- and relational dysregulation and post-traumatic spectrum symptoms. To gain a diagnosis, symptoms would have to be present for six months or more and be having a clinically significant impact on the individual's level of functioning. Sadly, it didn't get included in the manual, but is still used often today.

There is also some controversy and certainly a lot of misunderstanding about dissociation and the 'disorders' that are cited in the core mental health manuals such as the *DSM-5* (APA 2013) and so the majority of people struggling with the symptoms described in this book have been diagnosed with other things, such as borderline personality disorder, bipolar disorder, ADHD, conduct disorders, ODD and others. There has been controversy over this field for years, but a recovery framework is a well-trodden path that explains some of the behaviour, memory confusions, survival and protective behaviours and offers hope of change. In Appendix 1 I have provided some links to important research papers that evidence some aspects of dissociation and some helpful resources to further aid your learning, depending on whether you are a professional or a parent. Currently, complex dissociation is not studied in most counselling, psychology or psychiatry training courses and as such remains an area where few are confident to help those with these symptoms.

When the word 'child' is used, I am speaking about young people, youth and children who are under 18.

Chapter One

EXPLORING TRAUMA AND SYMPTOMS OF TRAUMA

Complex trauma in a simple guide

Writing this book is a little bit like writing a Simple Guide to Effective Heart Surgery! In the same way that the book would need to be aimed at qualified surgeons, this is aimed at equipping qualified and experienced psychotherapists and psychologists with the knowledge they need in order to facilitate a recovery process. The process needs a qualified surgeon or – in the case of trauma – a qualified clinician. However, recovery is not possible without the essential roles of parents, carers and other attachment relationships. In this book, I have tried to describe as simply as possible what the problem is, what the recovery process looks like and what is needed so that the environment for recovery is appropriate and the relationships are such that recovery is possible. However, it is inevitably a little less than simple at times, so if you struggle, I suggest you read about the basics in *The Simple Guide to Child Trauma* which complements this book.

This book aims to help you, the reader, to understand some of the impact of complex trauma and how to help a child or young person who is now experiencing trauma symptoms, such as dissociation. It's not a light subject to read about, so well done to you for trying to be that supportive friend or relative or caring adult who wants to make a difference in the life of a child. If you are a young person reading this, I want more than anything for you to have a sense of hope that things can change and the turmoil and pain won't last forever. I really hope the book helps you all!

Assessing trauma

Trauma can be defined as any experience or repeated experience where the child feels terrified, powerless and overwhelmed and challenges their capacity to cope. It leaves an imprint on the person's nervous system, emotions, body, behaviours, learning and relationships. What is traumatic for one individual may not be traumatic for another, but the degree of impact of the trauma is usually connected to the child's ability to find comfort and reassurance from a safe and known adult in the aftermath of the experience.

We recognise that many children are unable to find that emotional connection and safe place with their key adult for numerous reasons, including the adult being unavailable or threats or terror of what may happen. The trauma recovery-focused culture is one where we recognise that we can't make assumptions and we will never shame or blame anyone, because we don't know what was going on for them.

Children and young people who are exposed to experiences that cause such terror, powerlessness and overwhelm often have to develop creative ways of coping and surviving, many of which can last longer than the traumatic experiences.

Ultimately all humans are wired to try and keep safe and to keep away from terrifying experiences. What we see in responses to complex trauma is that when the child cannot stay safe or stay distant from the trauma physically, they have to remove themselves psychologically. These coping mechanisms can sometimes be harder to notice, because if we look at the current situation without an understanding of trauma, their behaviour just doesn't seem to be linked to any traumatic experience because there is often no conversation occurring about anything awful that has taken place.

It is essential when using the word 'trauma' to first reflect on what happened to the child and how it impacted them, because to use the term 'trauma' to cover the whole range of different bad experiences and the child's reaction to them does not enable us to explore the different levels of severity of overwhelm and terror.

Too many children receive emotional or mental health provision that does not take into account the presence of complex dissociation and therefore will probably not help the child in the longer term. Our approach always needs to be recovery-focused and not management-focused, or the focus is actually on us and our capacity, not on the child's long-term health. A recovery-focused framework offers hope for recovery!

Understanding the trauma continuum

The trauma continuum can help all those who work with children to use a common language, which consequently enables a child to receive appropriate interventions that are suitable for their level of traumatic response. The trauma continuum is shown below:

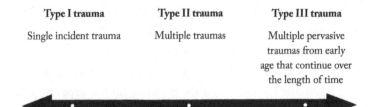

Type I trauma	**Type II trauma**	**Type III trauma**
Single incident trauma	Multiple traumas	Multiple pervasive traumas from early age that continue over the length of time

FIGURE 1.1: THE TRAUMA CONTINUUM
©BETSY DE THIERRY (2015)

The trauma continuum needs to be considered together with the parenting or environmental capacity continuum, which illustrates how great the impact of a traumatic experience may be. The parenting capacity or environmental capacity continuum for the traumatised child is shown below:

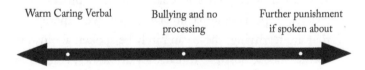

Warm Caring Verbal	Bullying and no processing	Further punishment if spoken about

FIGURE 1.2: THE PARENTING CAPACITY/ENVIRONMENTAL
CAPACITY ON THE TRAUMA CONTINUUM
©BETSY DE THIERRY (2015)

A traumatic experience could be repeated bullying, bereavement, physical, sexual or emotional abuse, domestic violence or abuse, an accident, a severe illness requiring medical intervention, a parent's physical or mental illness, violence, neglect, etc.

The Type I or 'single incident trauma' is usually defined as a one-off traumatic incident or crisis. Single incident trauma is difficult and painful and has the potential to cause injury to the child. This level of trauma, however, usually has less stigma associated with the experience; therefore other people are often responsive and supportive to those who have experienced these traumatic incidents and the person who has experienced it can speak about it. This would result in Type I trauma being placed at the beginning of the trauma continuum, especially if this was an experience within the context of a stable family where processing difficulties is a normal cultural expectation, as this could significantly limit the damage.

The continuum progresses according to the degree of trauma experienced, the amount of different traumatic experiences, and the level of social support and family attachment a child has to enable them to process and recover. Type II trauma involves repetitive experiences that are terrifying; these can rarely be spoken about due to the shock, possible threats, loyalty issues, confusion or a dissociative response due to the level of terror and powerlessness. Type III or complex trauma is positioned at the furthest end of the continuum and involves multiple different traumatic experiences that are serious, repeated and often started at an early age. They could be experiences such as a child who suffers from multiple abuse and/or neglect over many years (pervasive), without a setting in which the traumatic experience could be processed or spoken about in a recovery-focused manner, due to either the primary caregiver's absence, neglect or inability themselves to cope with the trauma. Complex trauma usually involves interpersonal violence, violation or threat and is often longer in duration. It is almost always an experience that causes a strong sense of shame due to stigma, and therefore silence, which can lead to the person feeling isolated and different. For example, repeated sexual abuse, trafficking, torture, organised abuse or severe neglect. (de Thierry 2015)

How is complex trauma different from trauma?

Complex trauma can be difficult to define, but it is essentially an experience that is ongoing or repeated or sudden trauma, rather than a one-off experience or a short-term traumatic period of time where there was a degree of emotional support, which would describe Type I trauma. Complex trauma could be caused by life experiences where the adults who should have been caring for the child were unable to, or hurt them, and it usually involves early experiences. There has been much academic discussion around complex trauma and a new name 'developmental trauma' (van der Kolk n.d.) is sometimes used to best describe the experience and consequent challenges. Sometimes we also call this 'interpersonal trauma'. It could be abuse, neglect, a chaotic home or something like a sudden, shocking medical intervention where the child is held down and feels terrified and powerless and the reaction of the adults is as if things are all normal. Usually the child's sense of being powerless is extreme and their sense of not being able to escape or speak about the experience is part of the overwhelming internal agony that leads to the creating of coping mechanisms such as dissociation. As a child, in order to survive in an environment where you are continually scared and your needs aren't being met, your brain's development can change and then how you view the world and yourself can also change. The challenge of trying to appear 'normal' and continuing with the daily requirements for your age as if nothing unusual has happened can be overwhelming and lead to all manner of behaviours that mask the desperation and overwhelm in order that their vulnerability can go unnoticed. Fisher (2017) summarises some of the experience for a child facing complex trauma:

> Feeling helpless, overwhelmed, inadequate, vulnerable, terrified and alone, the lived experience is that there is nowhere to turn, nowhere to hide, no one to help. The only resources upon which each individual can draw reside in the body: disconnection, numbing, dissociation, neurochemicals such as adrenaline and endorphins, and the animal defense survival responses such as fight, flight, freeze and submit, and attach for survival. These are 'desperate times calling for desperate measures.' (p.126)

The reality is that many of the children we are talking about may well be struggling with all sorts of behaviour that may look worrying, strange, naughty or may be hidden. Here are some examples of behaviour that are common consequences of experiencing trauma (Type I, II or III).

- The child may be anxious or hypervigilant, with sensory

sensitivities that cause them to scream or run when the lights are too bright, the car is too dark, the sound was too high, the rice was too grainy or the water too wet.

- They may be OK at school, but at home are kicking, biting, trashing their room, screaming, defecating and hurting siblings, or they may be displaying these behaviours at school too.

- They may be fighting, bashing, thumping, ripping, yelling, running, biting everyone everywhere and then crashing out and sucking their thumb and rocking but not letting anyone comfort them.

- They may run away, tell strangers that you are bad parents, call professionals and lie about you and try to sabotage everything you do to try and show them that you care.

- They may need a very strict routine, involving anything from eating food of a certain colour, sleeping with piles of clothes on top of them, sleeping in a dog bed, sleeping anywhere but in their own bed, not sleeping but tossing and turning all night.

- They may be behaving normally at school and then lethargic, in a dazed dream world at home, where they seem to have no idea of reality and forget everything.

- They may be compliant and be so scared of being naughty that they try and help everyone, say yes to everything and do whatever anyone says and then crash out with exhaustion.

- They may be staring at screens all the time and when asked to come off they hit, scream and go into a rage.

- They may refuse to answer to their name and insist on being called a different name and seem to be quite different one day to another.

- They may seem normal to everyone but have a façade that some can see through, which indicates that they are wearing several masks to hide the switching from competent to incompetent, depressed to defensive, sad to blaming, and to hide a deep sense of shame and rejection of who they really are.

- They may find themselves near drugs or substances that they feel drawn to the smell of and have no cognitive reason why and then they get into trouble because people make assumptions about them and it angers them.

- They may be very forgetful and not seem to remember important events, special trips or the day-to-day routines.

- They may be happy children, who then suddenly become a dog or fox or rabbit and refuse to speak in words but instead crawl, bark or behave as if they were that animal.

- They may be compliant one moment and then be controlling and aggressive and angry. The change can be very shocking and confusing.

- They may say they didn't do that awful thing when they are accused of it and be very persuasive. They may blame someone else for the event even if a whole class saw them do it. They appear to lie with confidence.

- They may be 'off with the fairies' in their own land and be staring into space but with little ability to focus.

- They may be eating constantly, stockpiling 'stuff' and stealing and you find little piles of 'stuff' hidden in their rooms.

- They may be depressed and withdrawn and then anxious and upset and they may hold their head as if they are in pain because of the voices and inner turmoil they feel.

The problem is these children have endured so much that has overwhelmed them and now they feel so powerless that they either act in (behaviours that are internal such as self-loathing, depression and so not always clearly visible) or act out (behaviours that are clearly visible externally) as they try and cope with the symptoms of still being terrified.

The Simple Guide to Complex Trauma and Dissociation

Silberg (2013) says: 'they have endured their trauma in isolation, but yearn to be understood, and hope that healing can follow from that understanding' (p.1).

Reflection points

- What behaviour would you want to add to the list of possible scenarios above?

- What behaviours have you seen the most? Which ones do you think are more associated with complex trauma?

- What is the difference between complex trauma and other trauma experiences?

Chapter Two

COMPLEX TRAUMA SYMPTOMS

Complex trauma usually occurs when a person is exposed to multiple traumatic events or when a trauma is repeated. In 2003, a group of experienced professionals wrote the White Paper of the National Child Traumatic Stress Network (NCTSN) Task Force on Complex Trauma (Cook *et al.* 2003). It explores the seven domains of development that are significantly impaired as a result of the child's experience of complex trauma. It explains how the diagnosis of PTSD does not capture the developmental impact of complex trauma exposure. The list of challenges clearly shows the devastating effects that toxic stress and complex trauma have on a child's physical, social, emotional and cognitive development. Although many of these can be symptoms of all trauma experience, they become more life-altering and impairing to those who have survived complex trauma. Here are the seven areas that Cook *et al.* have articulated and a simple overview of what they mean in reality, in the life of a child.

1. Attachment

When a child has been traumatised by another person, it will always impact their ability to trust others, be vulnerable with others and therefore be able to make emotional connections with others. The trauma impacts the ability to grasp boundaries, because the child has had their personal boundaries ignored or shattered and as such they can feel powerless, confused and insecure with other relationships as they try to work out trust and boundaries.

Fisher explains the internal conflict that many of them feel:

> On the one hand, they are driven by the attachment instinct to seek proximity, comfort, and protection from attachment figures. On the other, they are driven by equally strong animal instincts to freeze, fight, flee, or submit or dissociate before they get too close to the frightening parent. (Fisher 2017, p.24)

2. Biology

The body can hold the memories of the trauma. Sometimes the pain that the body can be left with longer term is directly linked, such as pain in the genital area due to abuse, or pain in the chest where the child was crushed. Whilst the child may not remember the details of the experience and so have no memory of the event, the body remembers and the pain remains, usually coming and going inconsistently, as if it is still happening. Very often it's the body that remembers the feelings that came as a result of the traumatic event, such as the struggle to breathe, the tummy ache and sick feelings that they were left with, the headache and dizziness, the fear of the dark or wrists feeling tender. The child may well speak about these pains because they are often not aware that they are linked to the trauma, but sadly adults can often brush them off as exaggeration or lying because the child can't say when the pain started and what happened. The child can also be left hypersensitive to smells, visual stimuli and sounds as they try and avoid anything that reminds their subconscious of the experience. They may become mute or lethargic as physiological and emotional responses to overwhelm.

3. Affect regulation

Experiencing trauma causes strong emotional reactions in the same way as you would experience strong physical and emotional reactions if you were hit by a car. Your reaction would be to scream in pain, cry and feel vulnerable for some time after the crash. Similarly, the traumatic experience leaves the need to scream, cry and wail in the depths of the child's being, but – because they probably would have been further hurt if they had expressed their feelings at the time of the trauma – they had to remain silent and hide the feelings, deep down inside. This leads to highly internalised adults who can struggle to offer ideas and opinions, and who also struggle with words. At some point, they need time and space to feel their feelings and to be allowed to express these hidden reactions. There are few words that describe the horror of betrayal, abandonment, rejection and being hurt; therefore, trying to have verbal therapy or speak about the trauma can lead the child or young person to be more frustrated or re-traumatised because they hear the hollow words that don't even begin to express the depth of pain. That's why art, music and creative expression can contain the expression of pain better than words and also why creative therapy is an excellent and essential method to aid recovery.

I often describe emotional reactivity simply with the example of thinking about when we stub our toe. If we are on holiday and we are happy and we stub our toe, we can be cross with the door and then quickly move on. When we are having a bad day, it can be the final straw and can cause us to question whether we should just give up and go home. Such is the life of a traumatised child; they are full of pain already and so a small, natural experience like stubbing their toe can lead to massive reactions that seem disproportionate to the small experience. It is also important to remember that some children will end up struggling with 'low' emotions such as helplessness, hopelessness, despair and depression.

4. Dissociation

This will be explained in greater depth throughout the book, particularly in Chapters 3 and 4.

5. Behavioural control

When a child is trying to keep going through the daily rhythm of life and yet has these massive rumbling feelings on the inside that threaten to explode at any time alongside body pains and sensory sensitivities as they try and avoid remembering the pain of the trauma, they can seek out ways to cope and numb all those 'problems'. Drink, food, drugs, sex, self-harm, adrenaline activities and in fact any addiction can be seen as a method to numb the pain. The older they get the more they seek something to help with the pain because help hasn't been found elsewhere. The child will look for anything that can help with sleep because that can be when the subconscious tries to remind the person of past frightening experiences. The child may well seek to be in control in order to avoid any feelings of vulnerability, and as such may instigate fights or other aggressive experiences where they feel powerful and in control. All of these behaviours are ways of seeking relief from the terror of vulnerability and the subconscious trying to leak into their everyday life.

6. Cognition

When the whole brain is preoccupied with trying to survive, it seems obvious that there won't be much room for the child to learn what seems to be useless information. The child is focused on surviving; anything else can be seen as in the way of that, unless focusing very intently on a subject can bring the brain a sense of relief from the internal conflict. There is a stress hormone called cortisol that can be pumping around the child as a result of constantly being on alert from the next danger, which can leave them unable to sit still and with extra energy that needs expending. Sadly, all these behaviours often get the child in more trouble and so the internal conflict is heightened again as they try and comply and please the frightening adults. I have seen many cases where children are labelled as having ADHD and medicated by professionals who do not know the importance of asking about the trauma history.

7. Self-concept

When a child is traumatised by adults that they know well, this can cause them to be in an internal conflict – they cannot hate those who are meant to look after them, so they often end up hating themselves instead. They are often left with a sense that they are bad children and that they caused the trauma to happen, and they can believe what these powerful adults said about them. I have written a whole book that explores the damaging nature of shame and this little quote summarises it as a consequence of trauma and all complex trauma:

When shame is experienced, it functions as an urgent signal that danger is here; the danger of rejection, failure, exposure and abandonment. It is an experience firstly rooted in interpersonal relationships. It threatens the very basic human experience of being alive and needing to belong, be loved and be accepted... Shame is different from guilt because shame is usually interpreted in the subconscious as 'I am bad and you think I am bad' whereas guilt is interpreted as 'I did something bad'. Guilt means that the child can usually 'fix' the problem by apologising that they did a bad thing. However, when a child feels that they themselves are bad and people around them think they are too, they can feel that they are not loved and wanted because they are bad and so a feeling of rejection can begin to form. This feeling of being bad leading to a sense of rejection can cause terror as they simultaneously subconsciously realise that they are reliant on adults to meet their needs and rejection therefore feels like a life or death issue. (de Thierry 2018, p.6)

Challenging behaviour

Each of these areas of challenge can often cause the child to be viewed as being badly behaved or naughty or not trying hard enough. With the 'trauma glasses' on, I hope it becomes obvious that all these behaviours are the horrific consequence of trauma that the child experienced and that now they are left with symptoms that they didn't choose, cannot often control and are equally shocked and frightened by.

Sometimes adults assume that a child feels in control and understands their own behaviour, rather than realising that they rely on adults around them to explain that the behaviour is a result of natural physiological and emotional reactions to experiencing extreme terror and powerlessness.

When a toddler wants to eat sweets for the three main meals a day, the adults looking after them patiently explain what would happen to their teeth, energy levels and health, and the reasons why vegetables are better for them. It should be normal to explain to children that when they get scared they have physical feelings in their chest, their legs, their head and emotions; and when they are very, very scared and powerless, their body holds all those feelings for a long time until they are discharged. It should be a normal part of children's education but currently it isn't.

We need to realise and remember that any defensive, aggressive behaviour that comes from a child is often an attempt to cover a sense of fear and vulnerability. When a child has been hurt badly by an adult, they often then take on the belief, on a primitive, subconscious level, that they have to defend themselves against all adults and we see that in their behaviour. The more children have been let down by adults mistreating them, having wrong expectations of them, judging them, being condescending towards them or pitying them, being inconsistent or ignoring, forgetting or withdrawing from them, the harder it is for any adult to get close to the child who is hiding behind that angry or dissociative protective wall. But we must try harder and with more skill and knowledge. Building relationships takes time but it can be done when we, as adults, stay regulated and patient and don't give up. It can be hard work seeing the challenging behaviour through the eyes of the child and their stress and turmoil and then continuing to show empathy; traditional parenting techniques can be like adding fuel to the fire of pain, whereas kindness is healing.

Primitive threat response

The concept of the triune brain and the primitive threat response is explored in my other *Simple Guide* books, so I don't want to go into detail now except to say that the primitive biological response to threat is fight, flight, freeze or flop and that leads to a decreased amount of neural energy in the pre-frontal cortex (thinking brain) which is essential for all reflective, reasonable, self-regulatory thinking. Whilst the fight and flight responses are more obvious and can be seen externally, the freeze and flop responses are more complex as they are internalised. The physical presentations of freeze and flop responses are usually misunderstood or not noticed unless the adult is actively looking for them; and yet it is those responses that are more associated with complex trauma.

Freeze, flop, numb and shut down

Freeze is a coping mechanism that is instinctive, primitive and enables the child to not feel, to escape, to distance themselves from the pain that they know will overwhelm them. It is not chosen as a cognitive response but is a primitive response to enable the person to survive something that looks too terrifying to cope with. Fisher explains the need children have to distance themselves from the event:

> In the face of abuse and neglect, especially at the hands of those they love, children need enough psychological distance from what is happening to avoid being over-whelmed and survive psychologically intact. (Fisher 2017, p.19)

The freeze response begins as a basic freeze where time seems to stand still and the body cannot move until the threat passes. This is usually behaviour that is more associated with a Type I traumatic experience – once the child has had more of these threats, they learn quickly that they must not look that vulnerable because a frozen person could be hurt further, and so they have to naturally create more complex, protective responses to the terror. The flop response is like a freeze response in that the thinking brain is not able to work and instead the body becomes floppy, compliant and the child can describe feeling a bit like a zombie. Or we may describe it as a rabbit in headlights because they seem like they are frozen, or like they are not in their body. Both responses cause the brain to focus on survival and so thinking and being reflective is impossible and the body goes into automatic mode. The thinking brain or pre-frontal cortex goes 'off line' in order to survive. Both freeze and flop are often dissociative responses.

Dissociation enables the child to somehow separate from the terrifying events and this is explained in the following chapters. These responses enable the child to either shut down all feelings in their body or emotions or escape into a made-up world in their head, where they feel safer. The feeling of being numb is not something that a healthy person would want to experience long term, but when the alternative is to live with constant reccurring turmoil, pain and strong, overwhelming feelings, numb can be the only option. Sometimes a child is so numb that they then can't feel alive; but it can be worth it to feel more in control of the strong feelings that threaten to 'leak' into their here and now and wreck their sense of power or 'normality'. Feeling our feelings can be threatening when a child is not used to it. Not feeling the feelings can lead to all sorts of problems like incontinence and hurting themselves.

Numb and 'switching off' feelings or bodily sensations or a sense of feeling alive can be a normal reaction to terror. Many young people have perfected the art of looking like they don't care and this is because if they do let anyone know they care, they may have to experience grief and disappointment when people don't respond in the way they need them to, so it's easier to pretend it doesn't matter anyway. Some children may always smile so that people don't question what is going on in their life and come too close. The smile keeps people at a distance so that the child's awful secrets will remain as such and further punishment for 'letting on what is going on' won't happen. I only wish that teachers, parents and carers could see through the fake smiles and see the terror in the eyes of the child smiling desperately.

The state of shutdown is another psychological, instinctive reaction to terror and is a state of total overwhelm when nothing else seems to be an option. It is not a choice, but a very primitive state where the body conserves energy and there is a slowing down of the breathing and metabolic resources. Some children can even shut down to the extent where it appears as if they are fainting or having a fit. It is a desperate attempt at staying alive in the face of terror.

The key approach is respect for all who have experienced complex trauma

For the child to survive something that is too much for their psyche and fragility to really cope with, they have to come up with methods of surviving and keeping going through daily experiences as if those horrific events are not happening or never happened. We have to first respect all who have survived these horrors, because when we are working with those who have experienced horrific trauma, they will sense if we are frustrated with them or pity them and this can stop them engaging with the possible positive human connection that we can offer. In order to have deep and authentic respect and empathy, we need to always reflect enough on the ways that the child survived. It's not easy for the adults around these children, but they don't want to be so difficult to be with – they just tried to stay alive. We also need to remember that the brain is hugely malleable in childhood and can make changes with far less effort than in adulthood; therefore change and recovery are possible and will be worth the hard work for the long-term gain.

Reflection points

- Which domain or challenge of complex trauma is the child you are concerned about most impacted by? What do they need?

- Have you seen all these behaviours from children who have experienced trauma? Can you see that they are natural consequences of what has happened to them? Which one has surprised you?

- Have you noticed that a lot of trauma work that is offered is aimed at Type I trauma whereas the more severe and ongoing the trauma experience, the less knowledge and provision there is for the child to recover?

Chapter Three

INTRODUCING DISSOCIATION

The window of tolerance

Dan Siegel (Fosha, Siegel and Solomon 2009) came up with a theory he called 'the window of tolerance' (p.223), which is used to describe how children who have not experienced trauma can almost always stay within a normal range in their behaviour and emotions, or stay within 'the window'. If you picture a window, imagine that above the window is a similar shape and size that represents all the hyperasousal behaviours, and below the window is another similar shape and size which represents the hypoarousal behaviours. In healthy children the window is large in size as they only occasionally peak into hyperarousal and dip into hypoarousal, but for children who have been traumatised, they may have a small window and the other parts are larger. Siegel describes how when the child has been traumatised, however, they may spend little time within that 'window' and much more time in behaviour and emotions that are hyperaroused (top of the window) such as aggression, running, fighting, being emotionally reactive, hypervigilant (looking/smelling/listening for the next danger to happen), being agitated and restless. Alternatively, they may spend time in hypoaroused behaviours (bottom of the window) where they are dissociative, lethargic, compliant, in a daze, with numbed emotions or inattentive.

All of these behaviours are therefore seen as symptoms of trauma. So rather than looking at these from a medical model (which tends to ask 'What is wrong with them?'), we look at what happened to the child and see that they are reacting to that in a defensive way. So – in the same way that if you put your fingers into a plug socket, your reaction would be one of shock, pain and terror as an electrical current went through you – these behaviours or trauma symptoms are due to the child feeling terror and powerlessness and needing some help from a calm and safe adult to process and make sense of the experiences. When we understand the different reactions to trauma, we can provide calm when the child is hyperaroused and provide activation when the child is hypoaroused.

Trauma symptoms left without support

If the child is not able to have a consistent relationship with a safe, calm adult who can offer predictable, kind, nurturing, repetitive help following multiple trauma experiences, then the child may become a young person who has a subconscious instinct to discover new ways of coping with these different hyper- or hypoarousal symptoms and as such they can end up experimenting with drugs, drink, self-harming, sex or binge-watching TV. The aim would be to numb themselves from the pain and turmoil because it seems like the only option to stay alive and no one has enabled them to understand that numbing only covers the pain and doesn't resolve it. Resolve only comes through a therapeutic, kind adult – preferably the primary attachment figure alongside a professional clinician, who can give strength to the young person to face what their subconscious wants to deny and begin to unpack the hidden story of what happened that frightened them so much.

Even with the most strong denial or dissociative response to the trauma, the body usually speaks about the pain and overwhelm but without words. We need to be curious about all body pains and challenges. Healing from the impact of trauma and dissociation is only possible when the child or adult is courageous enough and supported enough to begin slowly to explore the pain that lies buried in the body and subconscious. Often a child who has experienced complex trauma will be someone who still has to try and cope with, and sometimes hide, their reactions to experiences. The more the child was left on their own or with a fragile or ill parent or with emotionally distant or frightening parents, the more the child will not be able to make sense of why they feel so different.

Sometimes I feel like it's all a dream and not real. Like I'm watching myself from outside my own body. Sometimes I feel a part of my body numbs and I can't control it or feel it. (Sam, aged 13)

Misunderstanding and understanding dissociation

Hyperarousal (acting out) behaviours are more understood by professionals working with traumatised children because they can see them clearly and the child can often be disruptive. Hypoarousal (acting in) behaviours are often less understood by professionals and yet are a big part of the symptoms of complex trauma. Dissociation is a common hypoarousal symptom. A lot of professionals refer to dissociation as zoning out or daydreaming when the child should be focusing on a task. It is often spoken about as not being grounded or 'in the here and now', and therefore many people are practising being 'in the present' with simple exercises to help them. Not being in the present or the here and now can indeed be a dissociative response, but dissociation is more complex than that. Sadly, in my experience, there seems to be little understanding of or reference to the breadth of possibilities of behaviours that could be called dissociative in many trauma-aware interventions and, thus, the children who have experienced the very worst of trauma are usually misunderstood or, worse still, ignored. This can lead to the child sometimes playing a sort of game in therapy, trying to guess what to say in order to stay in control, using the time to constantly hide their vulnerability and instead continuing to strengthen the dissociative walls that protect and cover the secret turmoil and pain that no one must see. Thus, many children 'go through therapy' and can even look surprised if the reasons for the therapy are stated, leading the therapist to co-operate rather than challenge the dissociation and protecting mechanisms. Having supervised and trained many child psychotherapists, I have found that a completely non-directive approach in therapy with a child who has experienced complex trauma does not often seem to work for this reason, except whilst building the therapeutic relationship.

Dissociation is a way of separating or distancing in order to survive. It is a biological survival mechanism and a psychological defence system.

Putnam (1997) says that 'dissociation is often conceptualised as a defensive process that protects the individual in the face of overwhelming trauma' (p.75). A person can experience being disconnected from themselves, including their memories, feelings, actions, thoughts, body and even their identity. For some people, this could be a short-term survival strategy that is useful to survive a crisis and is not used again, but in this book we want to explore the coping mechanism that can persist for months, years, or a lifetime and often way after it was needed as a survival mechanism. Many children not only dissociate during the traumatic event but also anytime they are reminded about that event.

For example, if a child was kicked by a horse, then they may recover, but every time they see a horse, or they see a picture of a horse, or someone wears a coat that smells of a horse or farm, they may have the same reactions as if they are being kicked again. They may not associate their reaction with the horse experience and wonder why they are reacting so dramatically for what seems like 'no reason'. Dissociation can allow the person to compartmentalise and disconnect from aspects of traumatic experiences that could otherwise overwhelm their capacity to cope. It enables the traumatic memories to be kept far away from the core self, but becomes a dysfunctional coping mechanism that causes all sorts of problems.

The dissociation continuum

There is a dissociation continuum that enables us to explore the different levels of severity of this coping mechanism. Mild dissociation can be referred to as 'spacing out' or not being present, and occasional, intentional use need not be a massive problem; however, we need to watch out for any growing dependency on it as a method to avoid something, as this would be concerning. Dissociation for extended periods of time can lead to more serious mental health problems for the individual, hence the earlier this is addressed the better. Also, the longer dissociation is active in the life of the child, the more it might interfere in the child's general day-to-day functioning. It might inhibit taking responsibility for self or tasks at home, or with complying with requests at home and/or school. It might cause disruption in learning;

for example, the child might be present at times and hear important information in the class and at other times they might be absent and missing crucial information. Dissociation might also impact on all relationships – for example, attachments to parents, relationships to family, friends, peers due to taking too much control, or being too passive and complaint, or being too demanding and aggressive, or being too withdrawn. It might also 'steal' many hours of sleep for the child, create uncomfortable demands on food preferences, clothes, etc.

Normal dissociation   Depersonalisation   DID
                                Derealisation

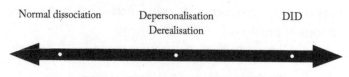

Other specified dissociative disorders (OSDD)

FIGURE 3.1: DISSOCIATION CONTINUUM

In moderate dissociation the child has learned to block out, switch off or separate themselves from unpleasant sensations, experiences or feelings in order to continue to function in daily life. Sometimes this can lead people to be 'in their heads' and very knowledgable and intelligent, where all feelings are analysed rather than felt, and vulnerability is hidden behind walls of arrogance and superiority. This can successfully keep people away from the vulnerability that they feel needs to be a secret due to shame.

Derealisation and depersonalisation are two dissociative responses that humans often utilise in order to survive a terrifying experience where they have no control or ability to fight back or escape. Not feeling their bodies and the pain that lurks there or not feeling truly alive and instead feeling numb or in a world where they can control everything can be a coping mechanism that helps them survive awful experiences.

Derealisation

Derealisation enables the child to block out the reality of the here and now and can allow them to escape in their minds to a place where either things are more blurred, more numb or where they don't have to realise how awful their experience is because it would be too much to cope with. The experience doesn't seem real and so can't be happening, so they create some method to be able to survive it without really 'being there'. They may describe living in a daze or they may be difficult to 'wake up' from a zoned-out space. They are detached from their surrounding world and sometimes speak about living with a glass door or screen between them and others. Some people have described it as if they were living through a camera lens rather than really living life; others have described it as if they feel as though the world around them is unreal, or some objects were changing in colour or shape. Some children seem to live in a fantasy world and although all children should have a great imagination, if they seem to spend a lot of time in that space, that can be a sign of derealisation and a lack of being able to be in the here and now.

Carly lived happily enough but she needed to spend hours watching TV or computer games in a zoned-out state in order to fall asleep. Often she fell asleep in front of the TV and then slept with piles of clothes on top of her. She often zoned out at school and struggled to stay focused on her work because she spent time going into her own world in her head. (Mentor of Carly, aged 16)

Depersonalisation

Depersonalisation is similar but usually indicates a response that switches off the emotional feelings, the physical sensations or some other aspect of the experience that is overwhelming. The person may feel disconnected from their body. They may not feel pain, or hunger, or being full or feeling ill. They may feel as though they are watching themselves in a film or looking at themselves from the outside. Obviously, whilst this is a survival method that enables children to live through terrifying ordeals, the subconscious often continues to switch off whenever the child feels fear. They can sometimes feel like they have no body, or they feel they are like robots, or that they are not fully in control of themselves. This can lead to self-harm, because they may want to see if they still bleed or feel pain. The pain can help them feel alive. Sometimes the dissociative response can be really problematic and harmful, as it stops the child being able to engage in the here and now with a full range of feelings or remember details of what has happened. When a child cannot read body signals such as hunger, danger, pleasure or anxiety due to depersonalistion, they can find themselves in dangerous situations. The following traumatic experiences can often lead to a dissociative and possibly a derealisation or depersonalisation response: neglect, parental misattunement or lack of emotional availability for comforting a child who is often distressed, sexual or repeated physical abuse, ongoing severe bullying with nowhere to go for help, medical intervention where the child was unable to move and was terrified, other events that were terrifying that the child was made to watch. It can be so deeply confusing for the child when the parents are present but not 'helping' to relieve the pain or discomfort when doctors are 'hurting' them and they don't understand why. To recover from depersonalisation the child needs to lean to slowly feel again using different body-based interventions that help them experience being in their body in a way that doesn't re-traumatise them. (This is explored in Chapter 7.)

Daisy was often seen running urgently to the loo and was always too busy to eat. She seemed happy enough but sometimes laughed when others seemed scared. She often looked happy and as her teacher it was a long time before I realised that she was trying to keep people away from seeing the pain that she was in. She was very fearful of adults telling her off and terrified of anyone finding out about what was going on at home, and so the smile was stopping people asking anything. She found it worked well at keeping anyone away who could pry. During therapy she slowly began to feel again, and as the memories came back she was able to tolerate feelings in short bursts and then longer bursts. She now feels and enjoys all sorts of sensory experiences. (Teacher of Daisy, aged 7)

Full buckets, overwhelm and multiple buckets

To explain emotional overwhelm to children, I say that we have two buckets inside of us: a golden one that holds our happy memories and a muddy one that holds our awful memories and experiences. If our muddy bucket gets too full, then we leak and our behaviour can begin to get us into trouble, but we can subconsciously create another bucket that can contain and 'hold' our awful experiences. Some children have experienced so much trauma that they have multiple buckets to contain all the horrific experiences that they have endured. Dissociation is a way to keep going in the face of continual terror because it helps the child separate the pain, terror, or overwhelm into manageable 'bucket' loads. Dissociation can sadly also cause them to be left feeling confused, feeling internal conflict and sometimes feeling detached from reality and like they aren't like others around them, but at least they can keep going each day.

In school Tommy would often say to me, 'At home, Eddy drew really well.' I used to ask who Eddy was and he would look surprised at me because it was clearly him. I didn't understand why he had two names and seemed completely different. His behaviour was very volatile and explosive. (Teacher of Tommy, aged 8)

Putnam's three categories of dissociation

Putnam (1997, p.68) says that he groups the defensive functions of dissociation into three overriding categories:

1. *Automatisation of behaviour* (Automatic responses such as fight, flight, freeze, flop, etc. When the person acts automatically and instinctively to try and survive and can often look back amazed at what they did.)

2. *Compartmentalisation of information and affect* (Using internal subconscious buckets or parts to separate out the difficult experiences, feelings and reactions.)

3. *Alteration of identity and estrangement from self* (A significant separation, usually with amnesia, of the self into separate buckets or parts that contain different parts of their life and can feel as if they are 'we' and more than one person – we'll look at that in the next chapter.)

Adapted from Putnam 1997

The subconscious

Many adults who are wanting to help children who have experienced complex trauma often try and work with them by using words and ways that demand the use of cognitive skills such as reflection, reason, negotiation, rational thinking and 're-thinking' things. The problem is the brain of a child who has experienced complex trauma is hard-wired for survival and they can't easily do those cognitive tasks without increased pain and discomfort, alongside feelings of stupidity, shame, powerlessness and frustration –

all of which can exacerbate the trauma symptoms. Complex trauma is a problem in the subconscious and the body. This is why cognitive behaviour therapy (CBT) can be most unhelpful with children and young people who have experienced complex trauma – they can struggle to access their thinking brain when they are triggered or upset. It's the subconscious where the trauma memories are stored, in sensory memory, and that needs the focus and help.

Experiencing Type III trauma can lead to difficulty in trusting others, fears of being abandoned or rejected, shamed or hurt, inappropriate emotional reactivity and the inability for the brain to stay focused on learning unless it helps with the overall focus to survive and stay alive. If the child has a safe, caring adult (one who is consistent, predictable, kind, nurturing and not a short-term relationship) who can help them express their feelings and explore their somatic reactions and internal conflicts, they can begin to stabilise and then eventually take steps towards recovery. The child will, however, always need some kind of psychotherapist to help unpack the subconscious memories and body memories because, even in the context of a positive relationship, for some time there are often no words that can be unlocked that can even begin to describe the traumatic events. For the child to hear the words she or he utters about what happened can make them real and therefore it becomes less possible to pretend it wasn't a reality; as such it can be terrifying to speak. Saxe, Ellis and Kaplow (2007) explain simply that 'traumatised children often have memories of relationships as riddled with conflict, strife, betrayal, violence, loss, and abandonment. There are a great many consequences to these memories' (p.87).

Flashbacks

One of the frustrations for the child who has been traumatised and the others around them is flashbacks. Flashbacks are sudden sensory memories that dominate the moment to the extent that the person feels like the terrifying event is happening again. If we were watching someone having a flashback, it might just look like they were being disproportionately emotionally reactive, because often silly little things can turn out to be massive causes of emotional explosions. The subconscious stores emotional, relational and body memories which become entangled and can trigger reactions that the child themselves can be shocked and horrified by.

Triggers can be sensory things such as a smell, a sound, a feeling, a thing they see or an emotion that is intrinsically wired to the traumatic experience in the past. If a child experienced a specific smell, sound, feeling or sensation when they were being traumatised in the past, it is only natural that they would be sensitive to those again because 'what fires together wires together'. (This phrase, coined by Canadian neuropsychologist Donald Hebb, in 1949, means that every thought, feeling, physical sensation and experience triggers thousands of neurons in the brain which form a connection. When an experience is repeated, the brain learns to trigger the same neurons that are wired together at the same time.) When a child has a flashback, the adult with them needs to quickly offer comfort, reassuring the child that the adult is with them, in a safe place and the bad thing isn't happening right now; the adult can then help the child with some grounding exercises (*see* 'What can we do to help the child feel safe?' in Chapter 6).

All methods to help a child stabilise and recover need to start by aiming to bring comfort and calm in the form of relationship so that eventually the subconscious enmeshed experiences can be untangled and flashbacks will decrease and then stop.

The lead professional

I often liken trauma to cancer of the emotions. Trauma causes toxicity to flow into emotions, relationships and the body, and needs specialist help to enable recovery. The complexity of the problem is such that the parent can often feel powerless compared to the training and experience of the lead therapists, which can add to their sense of powerlessness and therefore trauma. This is why the relationship between the parent/carer and the lead professional needs to be one of trust and a commitment to working well together. Whilst knowledge about complex trauma is relatively easy to access, it is complex and needs to be applied with great care; therefore summarising or simplifying it could be problematic and cause conflict amongst those caring for the child unless this is understood.

If my child had cancer, then I would read up and research all I could to be a helpful adult and answer questions from my child, but I wouldn't be able to treat them myself as I haven't got the appropriate training. This book aims to help you – the carer, parent or professional – grasp the problem of complex trauma or dissociation and understand what the symptoms look like; it also highlights the necessary safety approaches and environments that are important to enable recovery. It does not provide enough knowledge to facilitate the actual process, but I hope it helps you and leads to less anxiety and maybe further learning.

Reflection points

- Did you know that dissociation could be more complex internally than what you see when a child is glazing over or zoning out?

- Do you find yourself using activities or time to numb yourself from internal pain that you are trying not to notice? How about the child you are caring for?

- Can you see that when the child can be helped to slowly notice the internal pain, whilst it is tough, it can lead to a journey of recovery?

Chapter Four

THINKING ABOUT COMPLEX DISSOCIATION

Following on from the metaphor of the buckets in Chapter 3, it becomes clear why some children who have experienced too much horror or neglect need to create ways of surviving which include compartmentalisation or dividing of the horrors into secretive, subconscious buckets that keep away from their everyday existence. If the buckets didn't keep leaking in their daily life, I'm sure many children would be happy to store these memories and turmoil as far away from their everyday life as possible. Sadly, however, the child can end up living with feelings of constant conflict and overwhelm, often with no real sense of why, accompanied by many sorts of strange behaviours and memory problems, all because what started as a survival method becomes a dysfunctional division of the self.

Dissociation often experienced in complex trauma

We recognise the concept of having 'parts of us' when we talk about ice cream or a sticky bun! One part of us is very keen to eat the treat food and another part of us is persuading us that it is unhealthy! However, that is very different to someone experiencing dissociative parts that have been caused due to relentless and terryifying *experiences of trauma*. When the child experiences situations that are relentless and terrifying, without enough adult comfort, the child has to separate into parts, or what is called 'states' in dissociation theory, in order to stay alive and keep going with the day-to-day challenges that are set before them. This separation or compartmentalisation was probably necessary to survive, but long term it is dysfunctional and can be hugely confusing, adding to the sense of powerlessness and overwhelm as one 'part of them' (or self state) gets on with daily life with no obvious memory of the horrors they have seen and experienced, whilst another 'part of them' holds the details of the trauma. Dissociation and dissociative compartmentalisation are ways to feel protected from the horrors of the trauma and the emotions, sensations, thoughts and images that are connected to the trauma, but long term they just cause confusion. The more severe the traumatic experience, the more buckets or states the child can have or the more compartmentalised they can be.

The different buckets or states as a dissociative response is not a thought-through choice but a response that the subconscious creates in order to survive experiences that are beyond the natural capacity to cope. These responses are often due to the child being triggered by something that onlookers would probably not notice. The result can be an impulsive bodily, behavioural, emotional or verbal response that may not make any sense. The behaviours are often not age-appropriate and can make the adults around the child feel confused, angry, upset or frustrated, but neither the adult or the child can make sense of the behaviour.

Here the child 'separates' parts of himself in order to contain the overwhelming pain of emotions, body memories and experiences. These states can vary in how separated they are from the other states, and therefore the level of dissociation between them varies. This could sound as if it would be really obvious to see in a child which bucket or state is being dominant or presenting, but usually it is a subtle and well-concealed coping mechanism that only becomes obvious when another trauma occurs. Sometimes the child can even hear the different 'states' as voices in their head, and at other times it can just feel like an impression.

Sometimes children speak about hearing voices telling them to do something and they are confused. The voices can tell them to do naughty or bad things. Wieland explains that they can also be overwhelmed with strong emotion in that moment and feel a sense of total time freeze or confusion:

> The child may experience these parts or self states as voices telling him what to do or may experience a shift inside himself or such that the child is consumed with

the emotion or sensation or re-experiences the age that child was at the time of the initial frightening experience. (Wieland 2011, p.4)

The parts or buckets could be so separated that there is now dissociative amnesia. This is not normal forgetfulness, but memory issues that impair normal life because whole incidents or experiences have been forgotten. Some buckets can be unaware of the existence of other buckets. Dissociative fugue is the rarest category of amnesia – that's when people have such memory interruption that they can end up changing their name, moving area and taking on new identities.

The definition of dissociation found at the Institute for the Study of Trauma and Dissociation (ISSTD) is as follows:

In order to feel safe, the person needs to separate the emotions, physical sensation or experiences completely from her awareness so that she, outside of conscious awareness 'creates' separate parts of herself to hold these emotions, sensations or experiences. (ISSTD 2009)

Dissociation becomes an effective coping strategy if fighting or escaping are not possible options, as it enables a traumatised person to cope with overwhelming fear or helplessness. However, it can lead to an increase in long-term challenges that can be highly damaging to their personality, as it is a way of withdrawing from the outside world to focus instead on the inner world in order to survive. It should be noted that if a child is dissociative, this does not mean that they are currently in a situation where they are being mistreated. Dissociation usually persists even if a child is safe and within a supportive environment, and can continue until a child receives the appropriate therapy. (de Thierry 2015, p.90)

Sometimes I found myself watching what was happening to my body, from a distance, like it wasn't really me. It's like I became disconnected and so it didn't hurt. It was just automatic anytime I was frightened or knew I was about to be hurt. (Clemmie, aged 17)

Compartmentalisation and dissociation

When a child is surviving and desperate to appear normal, they can end up creating the separate buckets or states in order to stay alive (though this is not done in a conscious thinking way). This can begin as denial, so that it can take some time to remember a past event or even a recent experience, but it can develop into an internal complex system that can operate without anyone noticing. The states separate internally so that whilst one state holds the memory of the abuse, another state has no memory and so can continue to form relationships, even with the abuser, or engage in activities that would terrify the other state. The more trauma the child experiences, the more buckets or states the child needs to keep the experiences away from their conscious awareness so that they can carry on with fewer limitations. This causes a separation of the core sense of self with dissociation into different states, which makes life survivable in the short term but in the long term causes further turmoil, confusion and challenges:

> To the best of their ability, a child will make a dangerous environment tolerable; even if this is accomplished by fantasy alone. Sometimes this process involves creating an idealized mommy or daddy within the mind and dissociating from the reality of the external world. This can result in a deep fracture within the structure of the organization of the self. (Schwartz 2019)

To make sense of the development of these self states, I created the 'Daisy Theory', which helps children themselves grasp how they have managed to cope with traumatic events and stay alive, but has an entry point that is easy to access and is shame-reducing. The Daisy Theory is based on compartmentalisation, which can range in severity of dissociation. Putnam (1997) spoke of this as a defence mechanism: 'By compartmentalising overwhelming expe-riences and feelings, a child can both know that he or she is being terribly maltreated by a parent and can simultaneously idealise that parent' (p.71).

Below is a slightly abridged excerpt from my book *Teaching the Child on the Trauma Continuum* to explain the Daisy Theory.

The Daisy Theory

This theory is one that I have developed in my work with children and families to explain the way that a disso-ciative child has learned to cope with their traumatising experience.

In line with a psychological theory called the Watkins and Watkins Ego State Model, which is often referred to as the 'dissociation pie' model (Watkins and Watkins 1979), the petals are separated by thin lines that represent less dissociation between the parts, whereas thicker lines indicate that the separation becomes more significant and could be amnesic. In order to also include the structural dissociation theory of Van der Hart, Nijenhuis and Steele (2006), the middle of the daisy is often seen as the apparently normal part (ANP) and the petals can be seen as an emotional part (EP).

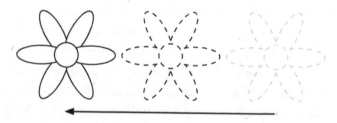

FIGURE 4.1: THE DISSOCIATIVE CONTINUUM

The daisy with the thick petal walls would be a person with amnesia between the parts and therefore dissociative identity disorder (DID), where the thickness of the walls enables them to continue to function although not as a whole integrated self. Previously, DID used to be called multiple personality disorder (MPD). The daisy model enables people to understand the dissociative continuum with ease.

The structural dissociation theory, which explains dissociation using the apparently normal part (ANP), which is the dominant presenting part, and other parts as emotional parts (EPs), implies that when a person is dissociative then there is a separation in the absence of integration. As the trauma increases and the pain increases, so the walls can become thicker and therefore the amnesia is greater between the parts: 'When trauma is such that dissociation becomes more extreme, the lines between the ego states thicken' (Wieland 2011, p.19).

Dissociative Identity Disorder

DID is not as rare as the media make out, but it is a serious disorder. It's also not as odd as the media make it out to be, although it is on the furthest end of the dissociative continuum and would be seen as a significant mental health problem. However, the child can still recover. It is so rarely spoken about as an instinctive, subconscious, survival response to cope with traumatic events that are otherwise not survivable, that most people would be horrified to think they had such a diagnosis. It is a symptom of severe trauma. Usually no one would notice on the outside what is going on in the inside and as such it can be tough to find out much about this trauma symptom outside of a trauma clinic.

If someone has DID, they would experience different parts, buckets or personalities controlling their thoughts and behaviour at different times.

- They may feel like they are several different people with different opinions and memories.

- They may feel like they don't have control over when these parts take over.

- The person may refer to themselves as having different names, and others may refer to them using different names.

- They may feel like there are huge internal conflicts, opinions and even different voices going on inside their head, which can make even simple decisions hard.

- They may struggle to remember some incidents or periods of time.

- They may feel like there is something seriously wrong with them and be panicking about that.

- They may feel like they are different from their peers and may be desperate to fit in.

- They may feel constantly confused about being blamed for behaviours they cannot remember and feeling in internal turmoil.

The definition of DID in the DSM-5

The *DSM-5* (APA 2013) lists the major characteristic of a person with DID as a 'disruption of identity', where a person experiences being two or more distinct states (or parts, petals or buckets!) and these states are clearly different states due to the difference in presenting behaviour, memories and opinions and ways of 'engaging with the world'. They also experience gaps in memory or difficulties with remembering events or experiences that took place when they were in different personality states.

Other parts theories

There are other psychological theories that use parts to help explore the subconscious reactions and responses but they aren't focused on dissociation as a significant challenge, so while they can be useful, they are not the same!

Memory issues

One of the problems that having many parts can cause is a sense of confusion around memory. For anyone who has experienced repetitive trauma where the threat response is repeatedly activated, the hippocampus (a part of the brain that looks after memory) can't put things in order and instead of an ordered memory, only the emotional, implicit (not explicit, so instead suggested) and sensory memories (memories held in the body and senses) remain in the subconscious and the client is not able to process or witness their own story. It can be almost impossible for a dissociative child to have a clear, ordered memory of a period of time, because different states hold different aspects of the day and thus no one state holds the complete narrative. Between the different states, they would be able to remember the whole period of time, but that would be dependent on the internal system working well as a team, which usually isn't the case until therapy has progressed. In fact, many children with internal dissociative systems are not aware that they have such a thing; they may not be aware that having other states is unusual; they may instead only be aware that they have memory problems, internal conflicts and difficulty forming opinions. Some would hear the voices of the states internally. This can lead to them feeling a sense of powerlessness and anxiety due to the vague or explicit sense of confusion around memories and time, which can lead them to be angry, further dissociate and shut down or use any other coping mechanisms.

Obviously this memory difficulty does not help when the child needs to give evidence for any of the traumatic experiences that they were exposed to, or when adults ask them if they did something that they have no memory of. The memory challenge can often lead them to further problems and they can be called liars or uncooperative.

> The child's internal self becomes disrupted. The perceptions, feelings and knowledge are still there – they have after all, been sensed and processed in some form by both the brain and body – but they are shut out of active awareness. (Wieland 2011, p.3)

When the teacher told me I did that awful thing, I really don't remember. It's scary. I would never behave like that. But now I know that I can't really remember that lesson so it's possible another part did it because I was triggered and didn't feel safe. (Chloe, aged 9)

Mapping the self states

In 'severe dissociation', each bucket or petal on the daisy is a completely separate self state. They are all individual parts of the psyche and as such they have separated in order to either contain a specific period of time, a specific abusive relationship, be a specific state that has a special coping mechanism or skill such as being aggressive or clever or sexualised, or hold a specific emotion that is overwhelming to contain within the core sense of self. At the less severe end of this internal dissociative system the states are aware of the other states and their uses, and this is referred to as 'co-conscious'. They can work as a team and the child switches into the most useful state when they need to and keeps switching all day (and sometimes all night) to cope with all the different demands on them.

At the more severe end of the dissociative continuum the child can sometimes be unaware of the presence of the different states, but is aware that they sometimes feel conflicted, confused and can 'lose time' (where they are doing one task and then suddenly can't remember what happened after that). Sometimes they are more than aware of their different states. The child needs to be curious about the conflicts that they feel and see that they come from different states. This can be a useful way of helping them know that it is possible to hold opposing thoughts in the core self.

'Mapping the daisy' (writing on different parts in each petal/bucket/part) is the first way to begin to help the child have a sense of ownership and power over their own internal life. The daisy provides a framework for them to be able to add information as they learn more about each state, and it also helps communicate that to the key adults who need to know too. Each state/bucket/petal can have its own time and space to speak, express and explore its needs until the trauma is processed and the daisy is not needed anymore. This mapping activity should only be done by the child whilst working with a qualified trauma psychotherapist or by a carer or parent under their specific clinical guidance and direction, because otherwise it is invasive and asserts a degree of control which is unethical without working together in a professional manner with relevant qualifications. Most professionals would need some additional training for this.

Sometimes I feel like I am floating and I can't seem to stay still in my body. Everything is in slow motion and I can't feel my body. (Sophie, aged 12)

Here is an example of a daisy that represents the internal system of a nine-year-old:

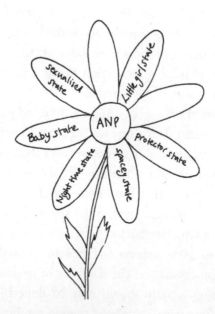

FIGURE 4.2: AN EXAMPLE OF THE DAISY MODEL

What becomes clear is that when the daisy petals or states are separate from each other and have thick walls to separate them with amnesia, the child has an inability to have a full memory of their life because the memory is held by separate states. This is obviously very confusing for them! Once the daisy mapping has begun to show how the internal dissociative system is working and then safety and calm activities have been found that help to stabilise the chaos, the next aim in therapy, with the family supporting, is to help the walls become thinner and the parts co-operate with each other. It is vital that the key adults start by welcoming each self state, including the ones that seem to have awful behaviours, in recognition that they have done a great job of helping the child survive. Once the trauma memories in each of them have been processed, they will not be needed anymore and the child can thank them, and the therapist can help them to integrate. The child can be encouraged to develop self-compassion for each state that becomes apparent. There may be animal parts who are there for a purpose – for example, to protect or contain something. The core presenting child and the self state will notice if the parent or therapist rejects any of the states. The states all need to develop trust and attachment with the adults who are key to the child.

> If the traumatic experience is contained in a self state, each self state may contain a distinct level of consciousness and a separate memory system inhibiting shared knowledge of the past and present. (Waters 2016, p.54)

Switching parts

As we stay curious and begin to 'map' the child's internal system with them, we can learn to spot every time they switch from one state to another. It's helpful that this is noticed and noted so that the states can begin to be known and what causes them to 'take over' can be made clearer. While sometimes we can see them switch, most changes just look like a normal behaviour because dissociation is about surviving, and concealing this survival behaviour is vital for the child's sense of safety. Only sometimes can we see changes in behaviour that could indicate a switch from one state to another.

For example, we might see the child:

- stare into space

- blink, eyes flutter

- have a change of voice

- change their body posture

- experience a change of preferences/conflict of preferences

- have memory problems/forget what they just said or did.

When we see the child switch from one state to another, we need to be curious and remain calm and consistent as they work out what they need in that moment. It's tough because the constant unknown is exhausting for the adults and also for the child. Tiredness then exacerbates the difficult feelings further and can cause more escalation of both switching and explosive reactions. This is why helping the child find ways to find calm and internal safety is absolutely vital. Many children do not switch obviously, but as we get to know them we can notice the slight changes to their attitude, temperament, opinions and relationships.

She held her hands on her ears and screwed up her face. Her mum and teacher were talking and they thought she was being impatient, but the voices in her head wanted to know what they were saying, wanted to defend herself, wanted to run, wanted to cry, and there was no agreement. (Therapist of Sally, aged 10)

States that are hard to work with

Working with any self state of the child that is angry, destructive or negative to the recovery process is hard. An introject is a state or bucket copying someone that has had power in their life; a perpetrator introject is a part that copies the behaviour of abuse. It's important to remember that the only reason they exist internally is to try and help the child survive, and they are doing it in the way that seems logical to them. Introjects mirror the abuser in an effort to vigilantly maintain the behaviours and attitudes the abuser appears to want, in an effort to try and keep the child safe. It can be hard to work with these states, but they are an important part of the dissociative system and need to have time to be listened to and worked with or they will remain secret and hidden, and the child will be left with significant internal conflict. They can't be ignored, silenced or told to go away; it is far better to listen to them and understand their purpose: 'An understanding of why traumatised children may mimic or take on certain characteristics of others, including the mirroring found in self states, can be explained by the discovery of mirror neurons in the brain' (Waters 2016, p.19).

Reflection points

- Have you seen a child appear to be like two different people? Does it make sense that it could be two different 'self states'?

- Can you see how shutting down or compartmentalising can be the only option to cope with continual and repetitive trauma when the child can't fight or take flight?

- What does the child you care for do when they feel frightened now?

Chapter Five

RECOVERY JOURNEY AND WHAT I CAN DO

Psycho-education

At the Trauma Recovery Centre, the therapists use the Daisy Theory to help children and young people who have experienced complex trauma begin the journey of exploring what is going on in their insides. What states do they have that contain the trauma? What conflicts do they feel? It is important that they see it as a clever way that their subconscious has used to cope and that they therefore feel safe enough to explore their states and what they hold. Our aim, however, is to help them slowly 'integrate' so that they no longer need the help of all these buckets, petals or states and can be a whole. In my work training psychotherapists, the trainees report that they notice the relief that clients feel when they can vocalise the internal conflicts and memory challenges that have become a normal part of life for so many of our survivors. They begin to notice when they 'switch' from being one state to another and can begin the journey of curiosity rather than shame and secrecy. The goal is always that the self states get to explore their role, purpose and memories and then are no longer needed and integration can continue until they have an integrated sense of self:

> What it had taken to adapt was a splitting of self and identity sufficiently severely that the individual's inner world had become a war zone. What I noticed was the relief these clients experienced as I educated them about dissociative splitting as a normal adaption to trauma. (Fisher 2017, p.2)

She was so convincing that no one had hurt her and she was happy. It was strange because the day before she seemed so clear on facts about the abuse. Now she was confident, calm and somewhat annoyed that there was even any mention of yesterday's disclosure. (Teacher of Penny, aged 11)

Primary attachment figure and home atmosphere

My *Simple Guide to Attachment Difficulties* explores the vital role of the primary attachment figure at more length, but the summary would be that 'attachment is the specific element of parenting that goes beyond the physical needs of the child being met and speaks of the emotional availability of the child's primary caregiver to be an emotional safety regulator for the child' (2019, p.18). It is also important to recognise that it can be really tough for children who have experienced complex trauma to trust adults and build an attachment relationship. They are dependent on the adult who is their 'safe adult' to take the time and patience to invest in them when there can be few signs of growth for some time.

The primary attachment figure needs to work closely with the psychotherapist together with the child to be curious about the behaviour and help the child find a solution to their turmoil. It can be an important shared aim to keep voicing that this is an ongoing journey and process, rather than just be desperate for the behaviour to be fixed. I explain the desperation that they can feel:

> The child is desperate to find an adult relationship where they can feel safety and security and from there be able to explore who they are and make sense of the world, but they don't have the tools to know how to develop such a thing and often don't know it's even a possibility. There is a saying that 'those who need love the most ask for it in the most unloving of ways'. (de Thierry 2019, p.60)

The home needs to be an emotionally safe place, so that anyone who enters it can be calm, kind and nurturing, with few unpredictable experiences, a predictable routine and as little tension and few arguments as possible! Recovery from complex truama is not a short journey and so everyone needs to be as ready as possible to be emotionally available and nurturing. The school and any other places that the child visits regularly need to be trained in an understanding of what contributes to creating a healthy, emotionally safe environment where the child can be sure that there won't be any shocks, surprises or pressures.

The stages of recovery

When a child is struggling with the extraordinary range of emotions, triggers, internal turmoil and other symptoms such as body pains, relationship issues, difficulty learning, and confusion, the process of recovery from complex trauma has to start with stabilisation. This means the child being able to have a sense of predictability, safety and familiarity in their living and schooling environments. If either of those environments is changing, for whatever reason, it is not emotionally safe enough for the child to engage in any additional work to recover because all their emotional energy needs to be focused on them surviving this further change.

Also the child will most probably have a running theme of experiencing powerlessness as a terrifying thing to try and avoid due to the traumatic experiences, and so whenever they feel powerless in any small way in daily life, it can be triggering to them and cause them to have big, powerful reactions which seem disproportionate.

For recovery to take place, the child needs to be safe in their here and now and until that can be assured, the therapist should not work on eroding the safety and survival method that the child is using, because this can be dangerous to their ability to survive. The dissociation that enabled them to stay alive is needed until they are safe enough to slowly heal with the safe relationships supporting and helping them. Once they are in a physically stable environment with some key adult relationships where the child feels emotionally safe, they will be able to draw on enough emotional strength to enter into a recovery process. Complex trauma is indeed complex and as such the recovery process does need to be led by a clinician who is recovery-focused and experienced in working with complex dissociation.

In that context of stability and positive relationships, the child can learn to engage in internal exploration, which includes learning to feel feelings that they don't want to feel (which we will explore in the next section 'Exploring the subconscious'). The child can begin to learn this art of self-awareness while safety, stabilisation and relationships continue to be built. Self-awareness is developed when children learn to reflect, be curious and then feel what they are feeling rather than try to avoid and deny the feelings. Then the trauma needs to be processed so that integration can take place and the toxic feelings that were buried or separated are no longer lurking in the subconscious causing problematic behaviours and emotional reactions. The next chapter will look at learning to feel as a stage before trauma processing, although the stages are not linear!

All of this should be accompanied if at all possible by additional support to enable the home and school to be an emotionally safe place for the child, and the key attachment figures should be spending time with them in enjoyable activities which grow in duration!

A model of dissociation treatment

1. Stabilisation and symptom reduction and safety.

2. Treatment of traumatic memories.

3. Grief and integration – exploring coping mechanisms, further memories and resuming of age-appropriate behaviour.

Adapted from Herman 2015

I used to make sure I wasn't there when they did that stuff to me. It wasn't my body. It was her. I was somewhere completely different, so it didn't even hurt and I don't really remember much, so it was a shock when they showed me photos. The person in the photos looked like me. (A trafficked survivor, aged 18)

Exploring the subconscious

To explore our subconscious is not a simple or easy task. It takes a huge amount of emotional energy for any of us to authentically begin the journey of being curious enough to start to explore our own internal subconscious; it is therefore a massive task for children who are traumatised and are still living in survival mode. The child needs support, kindness and respect as they begin to look inside themselves, and we need to recognise that some of them will have already developed a phobia of doing so. Most of them have avoided it for so long because they know it is where the buckets of pain, turmoil and agony lurk and they don't want to go anywhere near those memories or feelings.

As adults it can be helpful to use metaphors to enable the child to be curious about how they feel and explore what is going on in their insides, because the visual picture that is full of emotion and meaning can stimulate both sides of the brain and thereby enable a deeper understanding of how things feel.

Dissociation that avoids exploration

The process of recovery needs to be led by a professional trained in understanding the subconscious, such as a psychotherapist or psychologist. Despite research that has been funded to evidence that short-term, cognitive therapeutic provisions are adequate, we know they are not and regularly have clients access long-term creative therapy having felt shame and confusion by trying hard to engage with therapies that don't work with complex trauma. What happens is that the child makes improvements during the time of therapy but things don't last after therapy, because the deep subconscious was not welcomed into therapy because dissociation was not understood. This leaves many children and young people who have experienced complex trauma putting on layers of armour and a strong, defensive fronting self whose aim is to keep surviving and stops people coming too close. Or they spend years around the mental health system trying everything to find hope. Wieland summarises this beautifully and explains a massive cultural shift that needs to take place in our mental health system:

When a patient is dissociative, therapy cannot be successfully resolved if the trauma and the trauma effects of the dissociation is not addressed. And the deeply felt trauma and the feelings and sensations connected to it remain dissociated if not properly addressed and resolved. (Wieland 2011, p.80)

The team around the child

Full recovery is only really possible when the child has one or two key attachment relationships who have additional support and who can work with a competent trauma recovery-focused psychotherapist. Ideally there would be a whole team around the child in which there is recognition of the importance of the long-term attachment relationship with the child, but where the journey is led by the psychotherapist who has experience in helping dissociative, deeply traumatised children integrate and recover and is clinically qualified and has regular clinical supervision from another experienced trauma recovery-focused supervisor. The lead professional needs to have a background in understanding the subconscious so that the process is not overwhelming for the child. There is also evidence that 'the presence of social support has been found to be a very protective factor', whereas the lack of it can escalate challenges (Brom, Pat-Horenczyk and Ford 2009, p.53).

Unhelpful ways to communicate

When a child feels like they are being thought of as naughty when they zone out, lose focus, switch into another state such as an animal or change their mind about things that they were sure about recently, they can become more stressed. The child often feels confused about what is happening; but when the adult is able to assume that the behaviours are due to fear, they can work on reducing the fear and consequently enable a child to feel safe enough to eventually explore what happened. Confronting, shouting or shaming a child will only escalate the negative, protective, which can be dramatic. In fact, when an adult does shout or shame a child for their behaviour, it can lead to self-harm, self-loathing or anger and rebellion. It's also really important that no one tries to stop the child dissociating in any way because the need to escape from the intense pain will then become more internalised, hidden and more toxic. Furthermore, it's important that we never try to call any of the parts forward to speak to them, unless we have the person's permission to do so in that moment, because this is dangerous for their emotional and psychological boundaries.

Facial responses and tone of voice

When we work at forming those attachment relationships and emotional connection, the key is to remember that although words are important, it's how we speak and our facial responses that are important. It's the reason we like to look at each other when we speak, and why we prefer face time to phone calls so that we can see how people are feeling – we 'functionally wear our heart on our face. Our brains automatically interpret this information and our body responds' (Porges 2017, p.133).

Once our facial responses and tone of voice are calming, then we can make sure that we are also really listening well with our faces, body language, eyes and ears. We can focus on empathising rather than fixing or offering advice which can escalate the child's frustration. Children of all backgrounds can become really angry if we don't listen to them!

Empathy is the ability to stand in the shoes of the person and try and have a taste of what they may be feeling and then reflect back what we think they would need us to say that helps them know that we have tried to understand how they are feeling. We make sure we don't pity or sympathise, which keeps us at a safe distance and is like petrol on anger. We always validate their feelings, even if they are inconvenient, and we apologise for not knowing about the things that frustrate them. Empathy is not an easy thing to do; in fact, it can be exhausting as we constantly have to 'escort people into dark, uncomfortable places' (Music 2019, p.5). These are relationship-building tools that enable us to keep trying when the child is trying to reject us. They can regularly try to reject us because they want to feel in control when they feel rejected, as if they chose to reject us first. They can often push us to abandon them and give up on them, because then they feel that they wanted that to happen, which is easier to cope with than the shock of being abandoned. Porges has researched the impact of tone, rhythm and intonation of the voice (prosody) on the nervous system and it is extraordinary how much power it can have in enabling or destroying internal safety. He says that 'if you engage a person and they speak with very short phrases and their voice is not prosodic, suddenly your nervous system reacts to that and your body wants to distance yourself from the person, because now they are conveying cues to you that you are not safe' (Porges 2017, p.147).

Listening skills

When we validate emotions rather than silence them or dismiss them, when we offer a calm response in the face of the child's emotional volatility rather than get wound up and argue or fight their irrational responses, we are making positive emotional connections to them which are vital for their health and recovery. When a child is in an emotional meltdown, one that is reactive and raging, they cannot think, reflect or process information and so creating safety by offering validation and calm, alongside limiting any damage to themselves or others has to be the first response from us. If we show frustration or lack of care then the child can have no option but to disconnect because the child senses danger and 'as with anything that relieves intense distress, the process of successful separation (dissociation) will be repeated when danger reappears' (Wieland 2011, p.1).

He always ignored me and I didn't know why. He just wanted to play on computer games or look at his phone. I learned about really listening and so I made an effort when he was saying the odd thing about tiny, unimportant thing, I listened and made sure he knew I was listening and interested even though it did seem irrelevant what he was saying. I was amazed at the difference. He began to look at me and talk more and slowly he talked about things that seemed important. (Parent of a 12-year-old)

We obviously need to start more groups for parents and carers to meet to support each other in these tough times and all adults need to be aware how isolating life can be when caring for a traumatised child whose behaviour is volatile, unpredictable and explosive.

Listening is an essential skill to build emotional connection between adults when supporting each other and to use with the children so they feel respected, valued and known. Although just the experience of being listened to can help the person feel a sense of worth and value due to the time being taken to listen and care about how things are, it is so much more about our nervous systems being calm and regulated which is shown by our facial responses being warm and genuine and the tone of our voice being melodic and soft rather than authoritative and aggressive. One shift in the tone of voice or facial expression can completely change the nervous system of the child while they are in our presence. 'Listening is very special. Listening is a portal trigger to the entire social engagement system. Our nervous system is telling us something different to us. It says, "it's not really what you say – it is how you say it"' (Porges 2017, p.187).

Reflection points

- What are the stages of recovery for a dissociative child?

- What does the child's environment need to be like in order for recovery to take place?

- What are some key things I can do or change to make the home and school more complex trauma aware?

Chapter Six

CREATING SAFETY

When a child has experienced trauma, they either continue to live in a volatile way feeling powerless about their emotions, memories and triggers, ashamed of their behaviour and struggling to retain friends, or they have to process and make sense of big strong feelings and bodily sensations and relational questions. Sadly, many children are not given this second option and are instead labelled as badly behaved or attention seeking or useless. Or they are floating around in their own reality, pretending to be just fine and avoiding conflict and pressure. Every child should be given the opportunity to find safety, both externally and internally, and should not have to layer on protective behaviours as they grow. When a child experiences a single incident trauma and has an adult who can help them make sense of it, who explains to them how we humans react to fear and who comforts and reassures them, then the big feelings and scary new sensations subside. When a child cannot find that safety in a warm, consistent, nurturing, kind relationship – which could be for all sorts of reasons, such as if the parent were also traumatised or ill, or if they were not able to be physically or emotionally present or if they were the source of the terror – then the child internalises all these big experiences and they begin to fester and rumble.

The child needs their attachment figures (parent/carer and therapist) to be available to spend time (a long time) consistently, frequently and repetitively showing the child that their attachment figures can be trusted. The attachment figures need to intentionally spend time making emotional connection, so that then the child may begin to be able to explore their internal responses that have been festering deep down in the subconscious for some while. The longer they have been there rumbling and the more experiences of terror and overwhelm the child has had, the more explosive they may feel and the more frightened they will be of any exploration. While they cannot think too much, reflect much or understand themselves fully, the need for others to facilitate a sense of felt safety is crucial. Internal safety will take longer to find. Let us now explore what safety looks like and how the child is assessing their environment to find it.

Neuroception and assessing safety

A child will not be able to explore or reflect if they don't feel safe. 'Safety' is a complex word for a child who has experienced complex trauma. They are usually unfamiliar with the reality of it and need to slowly discover what helps them feel safe.

A child will be continually evaluating their safety and any possible dangers. Porges (2017) uses the word 'neuroception' to explain the way that our nervous system evaluates safety and danger. It is an automatic, primitive, instinctive process where our own nervous system assesses the safety or risk around us and then instinctively reacts as a result of the evaluation. For example, if we have experienced a house fire and we go to a friend's house for fireworks night and we are picturing fireworks in our imagination but as we arrive we smell fire, our neuroception could suggest that we are not safe and make a run from the house despite our cognitive brain knowing it will probably be a bonfire. Or if Becky goes to a friend's house and they all start to make hot chocolate, Becky may suddenly say that she is going home and pretend she has homework to do. It could be that she suddenly panics and knows she has to run because her subconscious remembers that she was always given hot chocolate before she was abused. Although she doesn't make the connection when her friends suggest it, her body knows and makes her want to run. It could be a tiny trigger such as a raised eyebrow, or a smell or any sensory trigger that alerts the nervous system to tell us that we aren't safe. Children assess if it's the best time to talk to their parents or carers about something they did wrong by looking at their face, their body posture and getting a 'feel' for whether it's a good time or not. Sadly, some of us adults can have a nervous system that is stuck in overwhelm due to our experience of life or we are just constantly busy or anxious, and so when we say with our words 'you can always talk to me about anything' our 'vibe' or our nervous system can seem to contradict that and so the child doesn't feel like they can tell us important things. That's why it is important to be aware of our own nervous system and our own sense of wellbeing and work on our own anxiety so that we offer calm, grounded, safe adult care.

I couldn't tell my parents about the rape because I knew it would be the last straw for them and things would just get worse. (Boy, aged 14)

The vagus nerve is the longest nerve of the autonomic nervous system in the human body. *Vagus* is Latin for 'wandering', which seems to be a useful description of this nerve as it emerges at the back of the skull and wanders through the abdomen, with a number of branching nerves coming into contact with major systems in the body including the stomach and gut, heart, lungs, throat and facial muscles. The vagus nerve from the brain is responsible for controlling the parasympathetic system and the Polyvagal Theory of Stephen Porges (2017) helps us see how the vagus nerve responds to experiences of trauma.

Porges' Polyvagal Theory presents our physiological nervous system as being in three parts, like a traffic light; we move from one state to another all the time. We are either in a relaxed social state, which is like the green colour of the traffic light and is called 'the social engagement system'. If we feel nervous or threatened, then we immediately activate our sympathetic nervous system, which alerts our body to respond to danger. This is our 'primitive threat response', where we feel threatened – a fight, flight or freeze response. It is like the amber warning traffic light. The third state is called 'the dorsal vagal state', where we are now terrified and believe there is a danger to life, so we shut down or we dissociate. It is neuroception that moves us from one state or colour to the other, according to what we notice in our environment that makes us feel calm and safe or panicky and frightened. It's not a bad thing moving into the sympathetic nervous system short term, because that can give us extra energy and confidence if we feel nervous or anxious; but we don't want to stay there. It is hoped the people around us will help us feel safe with their facial reactions and tone of voice and we will move into the safe and social engagement system. Human connection enables us to feel safe and facilitates healing.

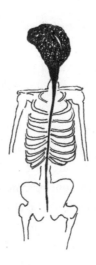

Complex trauma and neuroception

Sadly, we can all have a faulty neuroception, especially when we have experienced complex trauma. The nervous system is continually assessing safety or danger and reacting accordingly. For traumatised children there are so many things that remind their body or their subconscious of their unmet needs and traumatic experience that they can spend almost all of the time in a defensive state, waiting to protect themselves from the next danger. When a child assesses risk when there is none, then they can begin to create stories that can justify their evaluation, or they wear masks to help them feel defended as they continue to avoid emotional connection where they can't trust others. It can be confusing because their subconscious may detect risk based on a small factor that is no longer relevant, but the information is not cognitively available.

When the child has got a 'good enough' safe environment (it can never be perfect and without some stress!), it is time to get professional help from a psychotherapist where they can begin to process the complex subconscious that stores all the sensory, implicit memory of trauma, often in separate dissociative internal compartments. If the professional doesn't fully understand the dissociative system, which often seems to be the case, then only one part could experience therapy and other parts could continue to store the trauma memories, emotions and pains; therefore, the child doesn't fully recover despite showing positive signs during the time of therapy.

It is important to remember that the things that are comfy and safe to one person could be terrifying to another; for example, seeing someone smile or laugh or cry or frown. This means that we as carers need to be watching for the child's subtle responses to things to help them work out what stops them feeling safe. They can then be curious about it and move it from the right implicit brain, which holds unprocessed sensory memory, into the left side of the brain, which can question, reflect and use words about what is experienced. We need to be looking out for the child's facial responses, any change in their breathing and other responses, in order to try and help them.

What does safety look like?

When the adults around the child are able to remain calm, kind and consistent, the child begins to trust more and feels safe. Predictable, consistent, nurturing adults eventually enable the brain of the traumatised child to be re-wired to accept relationships rather than defend themselves against all relationships due to fear of abandonment and rejection. Safety is a physical matter and an emotional sense that is felt internally and provides a sense of hope. Often children don't feel safe when they are safe, because it can take a long time for the nervous system to know that they are safe. Safety for a dissociative child firstly means that there is a sense of team with all the states (often called co-consciousness) and they can all share the goal of integration:

> When parents stay calm and model empathy towards their children (such as empathizing with them how difficult it must be to have parts of themselves with such contradictory feelings, thoughts, and wishes) children will become less defensive and are more likely to calm down. In this way parents can become powerful co-regulators of their children's arousal and over time, the children may begin to mirror their parents' calm demeanor. (Waters 2016, p.161)

Creating schools and homes that are emotionally safe

Creating places that are emotionally safe is vital. An average child spends around 15,000 hours at school between the ages of 4 and 16; therefore, creating school communities is vital. In summary, a school trauma-informed approach is one where it is recognised that behaviour is communication, and that frightened children can be emotionally volatile and can disrupt their own and others' learning, or they can shut down or show increased sadness. It should be recognised that we are all complex humans who thrive on relationships. Here are a few vital signs of a healthy home, school or community that schools and homes can aim to demonstrate:

- Emotions are respected and validated and are not silenced. They are viewed as natural. Emotions can be less powerful when there is less fear involved in feeling or expressing them.

- We recognise that children need our nurture and care to be predictable and repetitive to re-form neural pathways that can tolerate and then enjoy relationships.

- A child will not be able to learn, focus, concentrate, play or relax until their basic needs are met and they know these will be continually met. Are they hungry, tired or needing comfort?

- Shouting and shaming are not helpful and can cause negative fear-driven behaviour to escalate. Any fear-driven behaviour that results from adults not being regulated is our responsibility and we cannot blame the child.

- All adults need to be aware that we nurture by our facial expressions, tone of voice, body posture, words and actions. We need to be consistent and predictable and 'wonder out loud' if we feel pain, etc., to depersonalise it.

- We recognise that children do not always have matching biological ages and emotional ages, and we will help them at the stage that they present with, in that moment.

- We recognise that behaviour is communication and as such will try and find out what the child is needing and help them reflect and articulate those needs when they feel calmer.

- We know that co-regulation comes before self-regulation and so we as adults know that we have a responsibility to offer consistent attuned, empathetic, nurturing, careful co-regulation experiences until such a time as the child can self-regulate themselves. We are all committed to learning these strategies.

- We as adults will remain adults and as such will provide positive, definite, strong boundaries that enable a child to feel safe and not have to take on the role of being a protector or provider.

- We as adults will be careful with our words and reflect on the impact of them. We will use words such as 'I wonder if…' and other phrases that enable a child to have an opinion so that they are not more powerless. We are intentional in using our words to build children up and encourage them.

- Tiny successes will be celebrated as we journey together and every change and progression is enjoyed together.

- As adults we will look after ourselves and look out for each other to offer listening, empathy and kindness. Little acts of kindness to ourselves and other adults can help heal and strengthen us as we work with traumatised children.

Porges (2017) explains that in order to create an emotionally safe environment we cannot separate the body and the brain. Our nervous system impacts other people's nervous system because we naturally respond to each other and need each other:

> The nervous system is not solely a brain independent of the body, but a brain-body nervous system. The future of interpersonal neurobiology is an understanding that our nervous system expands throughout our entire body and is functionally responding to the interactions with other humans as well. (Porges 2017, p.214)

Schools need to transform their behaviour policies to be relationship-centred, where the impact of trauma, the need for co-regulation and nurturing relationships are recognised.

What can we do to help the child feel safe?

Grounding is beginning to be more widely known as a helpful technique for everyone to do when they feel anxious, scared or about to flip out in an emotionally reactive way.

The elements are these:

- Speak kindly and calmly to the child and remind them to take some deep breaths.

- If they have had a flashback or a dissociative episode, remind them who you are and where they are and that they are safe now.

- Keep helping them breathe and if possible find them their comfort tools (a soft toy, something that smells good, calm music, a blanket, a box of helpful calming and comforting ideas as prompts for them to do).

- You can help them look for five things that are green, think of five funny names, think of five football players, etc. – anything that helps their pre-frontal cortex begin to come back online again.

- Preferably stay with them until they feel safe and calm or keep an eye on them whilst they are using their comfort tools. Check in on them until they start to move again calmly.

- Help them create a safe place with soft toys, good smells, helpful sensory toys, and blankets to hide in. They can then imagine this place when they need to feel safe when they are somewhere else, and remember the smell, feelings and sensations.

I like it here because I feel safe. I know I can say what I am thinking and no one will judge me or tell me off, so I am safe enough to work out what I am feeling. (Client, aged 15, at therapy)

Reflection points

- What makes you feel safe?

- What do you do intentionally to help the children you are caring for feel safe?

- What do you do when you can't process the strong feelings you feel? Do you remember to make time to process them or do you push them into your subconscious and then find yourself feeling a rumbling?

Chapter Seven

LEARNING TO FEEL

Safety, comfort and co-regulation

The adults around the traumatised child need to be able to be emotionally regulated themselves. This is tough when the child can be switching from part to part, is irritable, angry, aggressive and volatile. This is why each adult needs to be part of a team and work together to help the child. The adults need to be able to offer co-regulation to the child, which of course leads to them being able to master self-regulation eventually. Sometimes it can take an external professional to offer their hope and support to the family who walk through this painful journey. *The Simple Guide to Attachment Difficulties* explains more about co-regulation, but the summary would be that:

> co-regulation requires the adult to be emotionally available, present and kind, warm and empathetic whilst a child is having an emotional reaction. In these pressured moments, the adult is able to attune to the child's dysregulated state, bring a sense of calm and strength into the chaos and eventually, with patience and confidence, facilitate a de-escalation of emotion and behaviour. For an adult to be able to de-escalate things when a child is having such a melt down, it helps if the adult and child

have regularly spent time together with the adult being intentional about emotionally connecting through play, laughter and talking. (de Thierry 2019, p.48)

During the recovery process the child needs to be able to quickly access feelings of safety and comfort in their relationships, but also with sensory help, such as strong soothing smells, teddies, blankets and dens, safe spaces and music. The processing of trauma is almost impossible without the constant use of comfort aids that are always accessible for all the different parts. This can take a while for the child to explore, but it is vital work to enable the child to find safety in the face of the overwhelming grief and fear that they will be feeling.

Mindfulness in schools

There is a current trend for practising mindfulness in schools that can be quite unhelpful for children who have experienced complex trauma or who struggle with dissociation. Sadly, when a whole class or group of children are encouraged to take part in mindfulness as an answer to the mental health epidemic we now face as a society, this doesn't allow for the recognition of how impossible this task is for anyone who has experienced Type II or III trauma. The survivors of the most terrifying trauma cannot quickly 'feel' or 'reflect' on their breathing or their bodily sensations, because both contain memories of being terrified and powerless.

Simple breathing exercises can be triggering for many adults who have been traumatised, because they have survived experiences where they struggled to breathe and thought they were going to die. These experiences are stored in the subconscious and so the adult or child may not be able to remember the event, but their body reacts as soon as they are asked to do the task and they can immediately have a panic reaction. In a primary or secondary classroom where all the other children are happily reflecting on their internal state, a dissociative child will probably either shut down completely or go into a trance-like state, which is not good for them and evidences that they are terrified. Alternatively, they will take flight, or fight, or be agitated, or distract others by laughing or giggling or whatever they can find to dilute the intensity that they suddenly feel. In a secondary school setting the young person is more likely to swear and leave the room, looking like they don't want to comply, when actually they are terrified. Alternatively, they will comply and then feel intense powerlessness and increased terror. This is why the mental health interventions that are being suggested to schools need to be looked at through the lens of complex trauma and dissociation if we want to make schools a safe place for those who have experienced the very worst that life can offer. Porges offers his explanation that mindfulness 'requires a state that is non judgemental. However this would be incompatible with states of defense in which evaluation is critical for safety' (Porges 2017, p.236).

Learning to feel again

Many children have had to push down their feelings until they are out of sight, and so they are located in the toxic regions of the subconscious instead. Unless the child has had a primary attachment figure in their early years who has given them language about feelings and reactions to different experiences, they are unlikely to be familiar with what on earth to do with these strong reactions that they feel bubbling up. Having not become familiar with these normal experiences in their early formative years, they can often now be increasingly aware of the presence of the dark rivers of toxicity that they carry deep down inside themselves and feel fearful of them. They can also be unfamiliar with positive feelings and can find them threatening and anxiety-provoking. They can also identify feelings as that thing that happens in an explosive moment due to a trigger, alongside intrusive images and physical reactions, where they feel out of control and terrified, and so they can be frightened of feelings and what happens when you feel.

I find myself needing to do stupid things to feel. So I cut and bang my head and jump off stuff so I can feel alive, because otherwise I feel too spacey and I worry I'm not alive and it's all a dream I can't wake up from. (Jake, aged 11)

Interoception

Interoception is the process of learning to be reflective about our body and the sensations we may be feeling. There is some research linking how interoceptive processes may lead to improved disease and treatment models (Pollatos,

Kirsch and Schandry 2005). Other researchers have explored the relationship between interoception and eating disorders (Garner, Olmstead and Polivy 1983; Pollatos *et al.* 2008), chronic pain (Schmidt, Gierlings and Peters 1989), and somatoform disorders (mental disorder that manifests as physical symptoms that suggest illness or injury) (Mirams *et al.* 2012; Schaefer, Egloff and Witthöft 2012). A lack of interoception can also lead to or be the same as depersonalistion if it is a repeated coping mechanism of not feeling or listening to their own body. Depersonalisation is a dissociative symptom where the child has to shut down the ability to feel whilst they are in the midst of being hurt and then continue to use this subconscious strategy whenever they feel discomfort. This can lead to children hurting themselves in ways that seem extraordinary but make sense when we realise that they didn't have the capacity to feel the pain when it was less intense and so they couldn't stop the situation getting worse. For example, Sam couldn't feel either physical pain or emotional pain due to his trauma experiences; and whilst he was delighted that no bully could now cause him pain, he was also wearing pull-ups at age 11. He hadn't yet learned to feel when he needed the toilet. Another child I worked with burned his tummy on a BBQ when cooking with his dad, and didn't feel it until it had spread and become really serious, because he was focusing so much on his special time helping his new dad. These children needed to learn to be 'in their body' and feel the sensations that come with being alive without the terror of what the body may remember. It does not happen quickly and overnight and the child needs to lead the process as they usually instinctively know what they can handle. Sometimes the child can speak to their own body part and tell it that they are grateful for the job it did of not feeling but ask it now to feel. Wieland (2011, p.14) explains how 'the child's brain may need to be retaught (or for very early dissociation, taught) how to be aware of physical, emotional and cognitive responses. The child may need to be taught to see and recognize his or her body and body reactions as part of herself' because it can feel so alien to them. They can feel like they are an alien in the world, and do not belong.

Starting with simple feelings

It's important that we help children get stronger and more familiar with these new reflective experiences by helping them explore their reactions to simple, everyday things like the taste of chocolate or the feeling of crunchy leaves that we can stamp in. These non-threatening experiences can begin to help form familiarity and develop curiosity and then explore any emotional and/or verbal response to the feeling. Other non-threatening sensory experiences can be helpful, although we do need to be wise with some sensory activities that could trigger children with certain traumatising backgrounds. Silberg explains how central this learning is for the traumatised children we are helping:

> The process of accepting feelings, memories, thoughts or senses of self that feel foreign, hateful, enraging or frightening, can be difficult but is essential if dissociative

children are to develop central awareness and mastery of their behaviour. (Silberg 2013, p.85)

So, a part of the recovery process is learning to get stronger in skills of interoception that focus on what is happening inside our body. Siegel (2010) uses the term 'mindsight' to describe a process we can teach the children. It's a slowing down of the thoughts to notice them, being curious about the feelings of sadness or distress rather than reacting with fear about them and sitting with the feelings rather than pushing them down or running from them. The more the child can notice the dissociation, the less it will be an automatic reaction. In the interoceptive space, attention turns inward and, according to Porges (1993), it can be thought of as our 'sixth sense'. Children need to gently and slowly be helped to have the courage to be curious about their bodily sensations and learn to let their internal world be seen and validated; and in order to do this they need to have previously learned ways to calm and to stay feeling fear and panic without dissociating.

Children need to be helped to slowly feel again because they feel deeply unsafe in their own bodies as a result of all that their bodies have experienced. They often spend their lives carefully avoiding memories and flashbacks that lurk in their subconscious and bodies. van der Kolk explains:

> Traumatized people chronically feel unsafe inside their bodies: the past is alive in the form of gnawing interior discomfort. Their bodies are constantly bombarded by visceral warning signs, and, in an attempt to control these processes, they often become expert at ignoring their gut feelings and in numbing awareness of what is played out inside. They learn to hide from their selves. (van der Kolk 2014, pp.96–97)

Reflection points

- Why can it be terrifying for children who have experienced complex trauma to feel their bodily sensations and feelings?

- What activities can we do to co-regulate with a child?

- How can we make it easier to help a child learn to feel?

Chapter Eight

INTEGRATION AND STRENGTHENING THEIR SENSE OF SELF

When children have experienced complex trauma and are struggling with dissociation, they can be overwhelmed with strong feelings and desperate to live like other kids who seem to be enjoying life in a way many of them haven't been able to yet. Part of being a child is developing a sense of self by asking questions such as: 'Who am I?', 'What am I good at?', 'Who loves me?' and 'Who knows me?' Sadly, complex trauma can stop that natural process because instead the child is preoccupied with trying to survive, which is exhausting. Developing confidence and inner strength and recovery can seem to be something that is way outside of their reach when thoughts like 'Am I a bad person?' rage on their inside because of how they have been treated by others. I do believe recovery is possible but I also believe it's really hard work and that right now we need to train more psychotherapists who understand this subject and who are available to help guide the families though the mire of overwhelming volatility and extreme behaviours.

I'm hoping this book will help increase the hunger to learn how to help the families most in turmoil and will raise up qualified learners and hope-bearers who can show our commitment and long-term availability to all who need it. The reality of secondary trauma for many of the adults who are trying to be the key attachment figures for their traumatised children is massive and there also seem to be exhausted professionals everywhere we look who therefore can't be as available as we need. However, I still think healing can be a reality, whilst acknowledging that we can all just try our best with what we have.

Trauma processing

A central stage of the recovery process is about processing the trauma. This can, of course, only happen once the following have occurred: the child has been helped to find some kind of stability; they have been able to experience consistent relationships in which they have begun to recognise the feelings of being safe; they have learned some self-regulation and comfort strategies, having experienced consistent co-regulation with a key attachment figure or two; they have begun to learn to feel some everyday feelings and sensations; they have started to be curious about themselves. Then they are safe enough to begin to allow memories to surface. If memories surface before these important stages have been secured, then it is harder to stop the memories creating complete chaos, but it is not completely impossible to work on all the areas simultaneously. It is important to note what Putnam (1997) worded so well: 'Transforming traumatic experiences may also involve facilitating autonomy, control, and competence in ways that do not need to directly acknowledge the role of trauma in constricting or distorting these functions' (p.286).

The trauma needs processing with the help of a psychotherapist who knows how to carefully lead the child through, making sure that things don't move too fast and safety is always monitored. The emotions accompanying the memories can be massive and feel overwhelming to the child and everyone around them, and so it is important to work carefully with the right foundations of relationship, safety and stability.

A jigsaw puzzle put back together

If the child is in significant dissociation and there is awareness of separate self states, this process becomes like a jigsaw puzzle, with a whole picture slowly emerging over time. The adults are like anchors in the storms of terror as each new piece emerges, bringing with it powerful emotions and raging conflicts. Each new jigsaw puzzle piece is valuable and each self state or part that emerges in the process is valued and welcomed as the container of valuable pieces of the whole. Although the child will sometimes be desperate to destroy any states that carry more terrifying memories, the therapist and primary attachment figures need to warmly welcome them as brave survivors of intolerable experiences that are part of the team.

Walters describes this internal conflict for the child and the adults as more memories are uncovered:

Impermeable boundaries between self states are analogous to a house with many rooms but without doors or windows between them. It can take time to remove the barriers, but knowing all the parts of the self and having the child 'own them', as the child comes to terms with what the self states contain will bring the child closer to trauma resolution. (Waters 2016, p.194)

The aim for the child is that the self states/buckets can learn to work as a team with mutual respect until some of them, and then eventually most of them, are not needed anymore. Wieland (2011) writes: 'Sometimes, at the beginning of therapy, the child's experiencing of switching can increase as the child becomes more aware of internal distress and memories or more aware of her dissociation' (p.9). Sometimes during this time the therapist needs to create external buckets or containers (like shoeboxes) for the memories to be stored in pictures, words or art form in order for the parts to process the trauma and lose their purpose and eventually not be needed.

Integration of parts

The goal of therapy is that the child develops a stronger sense of self, an integrated whole self where they can navigate stress without needing to revert to old methods of coping, such as dissociation. The integration happens when each state is no longer needed because their purpose – to hold a memory, to hold an age, to hold an emotion, an animal part or a protector – is no longer necessary because the child is now able to hold their own memories, be defended by an adult, defend themselves and have an integrative narrative of their life where they can verbalise themes and how they feel about them. Before the integration, the story they remembered was full of strong emotions and unbearable experiences that caused intrusive images and horrific feelings, rather than a narrative which has some order and meaning to it.

Once the child has been able to integrate more, it leads them to no longer being so triggered by sights, sounds and feelings – aware of where they are sensitive but also able to regulate themselves and express appropriate emotion for memories or sadness that arise. The volatile behaviour that has been a part of their life, either due to aggression and rage or internal volatility, where they switch from competent to incompetent, from sad and depressed to angry or happy, is no longer rendering them powerless and further terrified. Instead they remain as one whole person who has varying moods but who is able to remember and acknowledge the daily ups and downs. They can learn to appreciate that while dissociation was a gift that enabled them to cope with some horrific experiences, as Schwartz (2019) articulates, it can become a 'well-maintained, dysfunctional division between the part of the self that is trying to live a "normal life" and the part of self that is holding trauma related material' which they would rather live without. Instead they would rather choose authenticity.

I liken the dissociative self to a children's windmill that you may plant into soil or on the top of a sandcastle. It turns around and around, which is like the constant turning and volatility of the child who is dissociative, but if the core became bigger and the petals smaller and smaller, it would turn less and would feel more anchored into the ground.

To build the child's core, we help them process the trauma memories and build up the core self by enabling them to find skills and relationships where they can flourish.

Mastery and identity

The child needs to be able to grasp their history and articulate in some way their story from a perspective of bravery and survival, not as a victim but in a way that makes sense of what they have been through. This then helps to form a strong sense of self where the child has a sense of history and a hopeful future. They can then enjoy finding out and being able to explore their skills and talents and enjoy succeeding at tasks they set themselves. They can move from powerlessness to mastery and their self-esteem can build up. Having been through the process of therapy and being able to spend time in interoception and self-reflection without being frightened, they have more self-awareness than many other children and can be quicker at recognising their internal states. They can be asked why they reacted in certain ways, as long as it is asked in a warm, gentle, curious way, because the child may be keen to find out too. There can be a familiarity about the process of self-awareness, and a respect and fascination for the way the mind, body and self operate, which can come across as maturity and calm.

Care about compliance in relationships

Compliance is one of the most frustrating symptoms of trauma, and especially complex trauma, because the child can be so focused on avoiding rejection and being 'good' that they push down their negative feelings as far as they can in order to retain an image that they have decided is required. When children are compliant, they can be seen as being extra good and of value to a class or busy lifestyle. The fear that they hold internally is of being rejected, unwanted or not belonging. However, I have often said that a happy, well-rounded child is one who has a sparkle in their eye, is a little bit cheeky and can enjoy the relationships around them, rather than exhausting themselves being on their best behaviour to earn the acceptance they are getting.

I remember being told the story of a relative of mine who, years ago, aged 13, was asked in a new school interview if he was ever naughty. With his strict parents in the room, he said clearly that of course he wasn't. The headteacher commented that it wasn't normal to be good all the time and he expected some mischievous behaviour. The child was shocked and couldn't comprehend being anything but perfect. This child went on to struggle with depression for many years as an adult. Children are meant to be full of life and want to have fun and play and be curious about everything. Teenagers are meant to be emotionally reactive and volatile as they move back and forth from being like an adult to being younger and needy to being more mature again until they are grown up. Knowing child development stages is key for having realistic expectations of behaviour and emotions! When a child is too 'good' all the time, the adults should reflect on why the child doesn't seem to feel safe. Silberg quotes a child explaining about the pain of compliance:

'My face is smiling but my brain is crying.' Through this colourful language she captured the feelings of dissociation inherent in her predicament. She wanted to please her father and the supervisory centre and smiled appropriately, but simultaneously experienced rage and confusion – her brain 'crying'. (Silberg 2013, p.196)

Reflection points

- How can you build up the child's core sense of self?

- In the process of integration, the key foundation to start that work is safety and comfort. What helps the child I am thinking of feel safe and find comfort? What helps me?

- Have you recognised a child being compliant before? Did it worry you?

Chapter Nine

DIFFERENT ROLES AND APPROACHES

The elements of complex trauma intervention

The White Paper that named the seven domains of impact of complex trauma also has six components of complex trauma intervention (Cook *et al.* 2003). These are explored in this book, although the language is a little different. They are: safety, self-regulation, self-reflective information processing, traumatic experiences integration, relational engagement and positive affect enhancement. It is good to see that many of us agree with the areas that need to be explored and focused on.

Working together

We also need to recognise that while it is hard being united as adults working together for the sake of the traumatised child, it is essential to have mutual trust and respect that enable us to listen and make plans which put the interests of the child at the centre. Often when working with dissociative children, the adults end up dissociative and fragmented when meeting together to discuss and make plans. The time spent together as adults needs to be focused on being calm and kind and building trust, with an emphasis on the shared vision that we hold about the child's health and future. Putnam explains how important our perspective is:

> one important intervention is simply helping others who work with the child understand the child's strengths, problems, pathology, and potential. If the child is viewed as too hopeless, too badly damaged, or somehow defective because of genetic and familial ties, there will be little recognition of or support for the child's compensatory initiatives. (Putnam 1997, p.266)

Looking after you

As has been mentioned before, it's so important to recognise the challenge of caring for and loving a child who is significantly traumatised, unless they are compliant all the time (but as discussed in Chapter 8, that can be a huge concern). Looking after yourself is vital, and taking time to remember who you were and are when you are not in the midst of volatility is important, although this is often at the bottom of the list. You need friends who 'get it' and a community where emotional reactivity is understood as a cry for help, not as the behaviour of a bad child or incompetent parent. Do try and enjoy some hobby with other adults where you can feel normal and breathe deeply. Learn to recognise your own shame or inner critic who nags you and tells you that you are a failure; and spend time with people who tell you that you are doing well but who will also be honest. Sadly, children are evaluating if they can trust you and are checking to see if 'their parents are strong enough to handle the intense affect and grief that accompanies the trauma' (Silberg 2013, p.194).

As a parent or carer, if you have got a personal history of complex trauma or dissociation, then one of the most helpful things you could do would be to take some time to have therapy yourself. This would also help you be the best parent you could be for your child.

If you are an exhausted professional, it's important to have colleagues around you who can remind you to look after yourself and put your own oxygen mask on before everyone else's so that you can continue helping others long term. Burnout is far too common and we need to be wise in knowing that we can change the world one person at a time but we can't fix the world on our own.

Emotional neglect as a key cause of dissociation

Evidence suggests that children develop dissociative disorders as a result of: being sexually abused, burned, exploited;

having experienced significant bullying; severe medical intervention; neglect or when their parents were not able to be emotionally present and their needs were left unmet and a sense of acute abandonment was felt (Wieland 2011).

The child is left creating different states that either hold different memories or feelings or ages, and these states switch around so that the presenting part is the state which is most needed in the environment in that moment.

For example, the state that is good at schoolwork (probably the ANP or well-functioning part of the child) may be mostly present at school until someone teases the child and then the aggressive state may become dominant and start a fight to protect themselves. Then maybe the child is told off and the state that is a baby becomes the presenting part and sucks the child's thumb and has amnesia about the fight but needs comfort and is crying. Then maybe the baby state gets some time in a safe corner with a blanket and suddenly becomes sexually inappropriate in front of the class and is immediately told off and becomes the aggressive state again. For those who are not aware of dissociative parts theory this can cause a headache as the adults wonder what could happen next and feel powerless in the face of the constantly changing behaviour and emotional presentation and the amnesia regarding significant events. The child feels overwhelmed and exhausted.

It is worth mentioning that whilst many survivors of horrific abuse have been reported to have experienced significant dissociation, I believe that emotional neglect is one of the most silent causes, where the child learns to live a life where they exist as several different personas all serving to help them be accepted and belong. It can seem to us that they are hiding something or seem a little bit fake but are usually really lovely. Underneath is a history of emotional neglect, extreme misunderstanding, loneliness and a sense of abandonment, but those things are hidden and a 'game face' is the mask that hides the pain and turmoil. Often the lack of traumatic stories in their life can lead them to feel more fake about their inner turmoil as they compare others' experiences. This can lead to further shame and secrecy about the level of compartmentalisation and inner turmoil and therefore can lead to the creation of layers of protective armour, numbness and dissociation that serve to stop them having to live with the intense emotional turmoil, but sadly also cause them to feel a sense of emptiness and confusion as they identify with trauma symptoms that seem to belong more to stories of terrifying abuse. Such is the silent agony of emotional aloneness and lack of emotional connection in their early years. Whilst the lack of relationships caused the trauma, it is also relationships that power the recovery process, as the child learns to develop emotional connection and trust with adults who navigate them through to recovery.

Grief

Essentially the child recovering from trauma will experience a sense of grief as part of their recovery. When the memories and feelings that have been pushed down out of conscious awareness begin to be felt and tolerated, the grief can start. It is part of the process for them to feel robbed, to feel angry and let down and to feel that their trauma experience has changed things, some of which will not be the same again. So just like recovery from the grief of a favourite grandparent or pet is possible, so recovery from the grief of a childhood full of sadness and isolation or terror and pain is possible, but only when the feelings can be felt and denial is no longer the primary coping mechanism.

Step by step

The recovery, integration, self-regulation and internal safety do not come fast. In our fast-paced society where relationships are often seen as secondary to living life by computer-focused, phone-obsessed millions, we can forget that things just take time.

Schwartz (2019) reminds us of the importance of each individual moment holding more significance than we think: 'Each relational moment of compassion might feel "invisible;" however, these meaningful moments are the building blocks of a foundation for a revised, healthy sense of self.' Remembering that it's the small things along the way that are important can give us the strength to enjoy some of those moments and endure the hard ones.

Summary: How to help a child recover from complex trauma and/or dissociation

- Stabilise and facilitate emotional safety in the child's home, family and school.
- Help parents/carers find support from a professional

who can support them and help navigate them through this period of time.

- Help the child find co-regulation activities to do with their key adults that help facilitate attachment, emotional safety and de-escalation.

- Help the child find comfort aids and objects and sensory activities that can facilitate a feeling of safety.

- Find a therapist that can stabilise, assess, map the internal system and then help the child process the trauma from the subconscious and body.

- Make sure that the family all learn about the way the brain works when they feel terror in order to reduce the shame of the behaviour.

- Make sure that there is at least one teacher or adult at school who the child can access if they feel scared and who understands complex trauma and dissociation and so can respond with empathy and nurture.

- The therapist then helps the child and family create an integrative narrative of their life, including the bad experience and what they learned.

Recovery from trauma specific to the severity of trauma

Type I trauma

The child needs an adult who offers a professional therapeutic relationship that:

- co-regulates

- is predictable

- is nurturing and emotionally available

- has a calm nervous system

- is able to listen and validate emotions.

Type II trauma

The child needs the adult who leads the process to be:

- a counselor or psychotherapist using creative methods who is able to do what the adult offers in Type I (above) but who has more skills because of their training

- able to offer a regular space to explore the subconscious

- able to offer ways to contain some of the big experiences externally rather than internally.

Type III trauma (complex trauma)

The child needs all the above for Type I and II but added to that:

- an experienced trauma recovery-focused therapist (not a 'normal' counsellor or psychotherapist but one who has attended additional training in complex trauma) who can aim to integrate the separated memories and what remains in the subconscious and body

- an even longer-term commitment as a therapist (maybe 2+ years)

- additional relationships around the child to support the process and add fun to relieve the pressure around the recovery process

- preferably support for the parents and carers

- the therapist needs to regularly use clinical assessments to note developments and progression and have proper clinical supervision from an experienced trauma recovery-focused practitioner.

Using our imagination to hope

When it is difficult to keep going with what can feel like relentless pain and turmoil, it can be useful to use our imagination to picture the child as no longer full of such pain and now able to self-regulate. This can give us hope and help us to keep going. Silberg (2012) even suggests that we can have the child imagine a conversation with an older version of themselves, 'maybe five or ten years into the future' (p.70).

The effort is worth it and the stories that you can tell of recovery can bring hope to so many others who are navigating this intense and difficult path. Well done to all the adults helping the children and well done to the children who are brave and courageous. I am sorry if you feel that it's impossible to find the right professional team, but I want to write what *should* happen for all the children who have experienced the horror of complex trauma and therefore what we need to join together and fight for.

GLOSSARY

Attention deficit hyperactivity disorder (ADHD) This refers to a mental health 'disorder'. People with ADHD may have trouble focusing their attention on a single task or sitting still for long periods of time. Both adults and children can have ADHD.

Affect regulation Sometimes called emotional regulation; the ability to be emotionally appropriate in different settings and not be emotionally reactive or explosive.

Apparently Normal Part (ANP) This is a name for the presenting state of a child, young person or adult in the structural dissociation theory internal system. It is the 'part' of the child that people usually meet first.

Attachment This word describes the crucial relationship between two people and usually refers to the relationship between a child and their primary caregiver.

Cognitive Behaviour Therapy (CBT) A talking therapy to help manage difficult situations by changing the way you think. It's a popular therapy method.

Complex trauma This is defined as a traumatic event that is chronic, interpersonal and begins in childhood (Cook *et al.* 2003).

Co-regulation Refers to the process in a relationship where one adjusts themselves when interacting with another, in order to help the other become regulated.

Daisy Theory This theory was created in 2014 by de Thierry to help children and adults grasp the concept of having several or many different dissociative states. The daisy acts as a psychological container for the person and those around them so that they feel less overwhelmed.

Depersonalisation   The sense of being detached from, or 'not in', or feeling one's body.

Derealisation   A feeling that one's surroundings aren't real or the person feels like they are living in a dream-like state or things are foggy.

Developmental trauma   A term used to describe the trauma experienced by people exposed to early and ongoing severe trauma. There is a set of diagnostic criteria developed by Bessel van der Kolk and his colleagues within The National Child Traumatic Stress Network in 2009.

Dissociative Identity Disorder (DID)   A condition where two or more distinct states or personalities are present and 'take over' the individual. The person experiences memory loss which is more extreme than normal.

Dissociation   A psychological experience in which people feel disconnected or separated from their sensory experience, emotions, sense of self or personal history.

Emotional Part (EP)   The 'state' or 'part' in the structural dissociation theory that 'holds' the emotional reactions to trauma in a separate state whilst the ANP is the presenting part.

Introject   Refers to absorbing into the subconscious the values, voices or thoughts of another person. An introject state is a 'part' which carries those aspects of another person and could include more details of that other person.

Oppositional Defiance Disorder (ODD)   A childhood disorder that is defined by a pattern of hostile, disobedient and defiant behaviours directed at adults or other authority figures.

Pre-frontal cortex   The part of the brain that covers the front part of the frontal lobe. This part of the brain is responsible for thinking, reflection, planning, decision making, etc.

Post-traumatic stress disorder (PTSD)   A type of anxiety disorder that may develop after being involved in, or witnessing, traumatic events.

Self-concept   Summarised by how we think of our own individual perceptions of our behaviour, abilities and unique characteristics. This concept forms a mental picture of who you are as a person.

Toxic stress   Results in prolonged activation of the stress response, with a failure of the body to recover fully, because of repeated experiences of terror and powerlessness. It differs from a normal stress response in that there is a lack of caregiver support, reassurance or emotional attachments.

Triune brain   A model of the brain in three parts, describing the prefrontal cortex, the limbic region and the brainstem. It was proposed by the American physician and neuroscientist Paul D. MacLean in the 1960s.

Types I–III trauma   Describes the different levels of severity of trauma. Type I describes trauma that occurs in a one-off incident; Type II is traumatic experiences that are repeated and prolonged; Type III is trauma that is multiple, prolonged and continual from an early age.

APPENDIX I: USEFUL CONTACTS AND FURTHER READING

Organisations which can help in the UK

The Trauma Recovery Centre – www.trc-uk.org

>The TRC provides specialised trauma therapy and training in several centres across the UK. The author founded this charity.

Betsy Training Ltd – www.betsytraininguk.com

>Betsy Training Ltd is the author's training organisation which provides specialised trauma recovery training across the UK and the globe. Betsy delivers training in large conferences, schools and many other organisations on trauma, complex trauma and dissociation and creating trauma-informed cultures. She has online courses on Complex Trauma and Dissociation at: https://bdtonline.thinkific.com

The European Society for the Study of Trauma and Dissociation – https://estd.org

>The European Society for the Study of Trauma and Dissociation is a network organisation for those professionals working in Europe in the field of trauma and dissociation. It has useful resources.

The International Society for the Study of Trauma and Dissociation – www.isst-d.org

>ISST is a members organisation that has resources about trauma and dissociation and a directory of practitioners who specialise in this field across the world.

Positive Outcomes for Dissociative Survivors (PODS) – https://www.pods-online.org.uk

>PODS is an organisation that helps and supports people who have suffered trauma and developed a dissociative disorder.

First Person Plural – https://www.firstpersonplural.org.uk

> FPP is a survivor-led organisation. The work of the charity is to improve knowledge, understanding and recognition, and encourage and facilitate mutual support of DID.

The Pottergate Centre for Trauma and Dissociation – https://dissociation.co.uk

> The Pottergate Centre for Trauma and Dissociation offers a wide range of services to professionals and to clients who may have a dissociative disorder, such as a DID, and to the public at large.

Childhood Trauma Recovery Network UK – https://www.traumarecoverynetworkuk.org

> CTRN is an organisation founded by the author to provide a network of clinicians, professionals and organisations that share the same trauma recovery focused aim across the UK. The website has a map to locate help and other resources.

BICTD training course: Therapy Training in Complex Trauma and Dissociation – https://bictd.org/dissociation-in-children.html

> BICTD is an organisation that runs training on trauma and dissociation.

International organisations which can help

The European Society for the Study of Trauma and Dissociation – https://estd.org

> ESTD is a European network of professionals who work in the field of trauma recovery and dissociation. They provide resources on the subject.

The International Society for the Study of Trauma and Dissociation – https://www.isst-d.org

> ISSTD is the international organisation with the same purpose. Both run conferences, training and have a network of professionals.

Child Trauma Academy – https://www.childtrauma.org

> Child Trauma Academy is an organisation based in the USA led by Dr Bruce Perry.

Further reading

Books for children about dissociation

Bray, M. (2015) *Rob the Robin and The Bald Eagle*. Whiteland, IN: Artsake Publishing.

Gomez, A.M. and Paulson, S. (2016) *All the Colours of Me: My First Book about Dissociation*. Evanston, IL: Agate Books.

Moses, M. (2015) *Alex and the Scary Things. A Story to Help Children Who Have Experienced Something Scary*. London: Jessica Kingsley Publishers.

Evidence for DID

Simone Reinders, A.A.T., Willemsen, A.T.M., Vos, H.P.J., den Boer, J.A. and Nijenhuis, E.R.S (2012) 'Fact or factitious? A psychobiological study of authentic and simulated dissociative identity state.' *PLoS ONE 7*, 6, e39279.

Reinders, A., Marquand, A., Schlumpf, Y., Chalavi, S. *et al.* (2019) 'Aiding the diagnosis of dissociative identity disorder: Pattern recognition study of brain biomarkers.' *British Journal of Psychiatry 215*, 3, 536–544.

Developmental trauma and PTSD

Ogden, P., Minton, K. and Pain, C. (2006) *Trauma and the Body: A Sensorimotor Approach to Psychotherapy*. New York, NY: W.W. Norton & Company.

van der Kolk, B. (n.d.) 'Developmental Trauma Disorder.' Accessed on 10/04/20 at https://traumaticstressinstitute.org/wp-content/files_mf/1276541701VanderKolkDvptTraumaDis.pdf.

Dissociative disorders exist and are the result of childhood trauma

Perry, B. (2014) *Helping Traumatized Children: A Brief Overview for Carers* (Caregiver Series). Houston, TX: The Child Trauma Academy.

Salter, M., Dorahy, M. and Middleton, W. (2017) 'Dissociative Identity Disorder exists and is the result of childhood trauma.' *The Conversation*, October 4. Accessed on 10/04/20 at http://theconversation.com/dissociative-identity-disorder-exists-and-is-the-result-of-childhood-trauma-85076?fbclid=IwAR2ipRpke7Moy sOFvXA2yYF9IHPdPHb39QUbiRhsCNWO-OD95gv-QyoyvkI.

Dissociative disorders are more common than people think

Kate, M.-A. (2019) 'Dissociative disorders are nearly as common as depression. So why haven't we heard about them?' *Neuroscience News*, July 29. Accessed on 10/04/20 at https://neurosciencenews.com/dissociative-disorders-depression-14589/?fbclid=IwAR1jzJUqsyrpg T7mFWfODfqFOP3-TMuIA0EJFyFuQgr3TdfOyMLVjtWg3Ys.

Schwartz, A. (2011) 'Complex PTSD and dissociative symptoms.' Accessed on 13/04/20 at https://drarielleschwartz.com/complex-ptsd-and-dissociative-symptoms-dr-arielle-schwartz/?fbclid=IwAR20T9 dphiTP_lheyqjlaeCuE28KxG6X9EO_jMA83nx57nZtQupj7DjdhSk#. XniVRy2cZ0t.

APPENDIX 2: CRISIS PLAN TEMPLATE

A crisis plan template to create with your young person when they are feeling calm, to be ready for when they have a low period/crisis or suicidal thoughts:

What can I do right now to distract or comfort me?

_____

_____

_____

_____

What could I do to focus on something positive or fun?

_____

_____

_____

_____

Is there something that would make me safer?

_____

_____

_____

_____

Who can I contact to support me?

_____

_____

_____

_____

Which professional can I contact?

_____

_____

_____

_____

Emergency numbers for professionals:

_____

_____

_____

_____

REFERENCES

American Psychiatric Association (APA) (2013) *Diagnostic and Statistical Manual of Mental Disorders, Fifth edition (DSM-5)*. Washington, DC: APA.

Bowlby, J. (1969) *Attachment and Loss, Vol. 1: Attachment*. London: Hogarth.

Brom, D., Pat-Horenczyk, R. and Ford, J. (2009) *Treating Traumatised Children. Risk, Resilience, Recovery*. Hove: Routledge.

Cook, A., Blaustein, M., Spinazzola, J. and van der Kolk, B. (eds) (2003) 'Complex trauma in children and adolescents.' *National Child Traumatic Stress Network*. Accessed on 26/11/19 at https://www.nctsn.org/sites/default/files/resources/complex_trauma_in_children_and_adolescents.pdf.

de Thierry, B. (2015) *Teaching the Child on the Trauma Continuum*. London: Grosvenor House.

de Thierry, B. (2018) *The Simple Guide to Understanding Shame in Children*. London: Jessica Kingsley Publishers.

de Thierry, B. (2019) *The Simple Guide to Attachment Difficulties*. London: Jessica Kingsley Publishers.

Fisher, J. (2017) *Healing the Fragmented Selves of Trauma Survivors. Overcoming Self-Alienation*. New York, NY: Routledge.

Fosha, D., Siegel, D. and Solomon, M. (eds) (2009) *The Healing Power of Emotion: Affective Neuroscience, Development and Clinical Practice* (Norton Series on Interpersonal Neurobiology). New York, NY: W.W. Norton & Company.

Garner, D.M., Olmstead, M.P. and Polivy, J. (1983) 'Development and validation of a multidimensional eating disorder inventory for anorexia nervosa and bulimia.' *International Journal of Eating Disorders 2*, 15–34.

Herman, J. (2015) *Trauma and Recovery: The Aftermath of Violence—From Domestic Abuse to Political Terror*. New York, NY: Basic Books.

Institute for the Study of Trauma and Dissociation (ISSTD) (2009) 'FAQs for teachers.' Accessed on 26/03/20 at www.isst-d.org/resources/faqs-for-teachers.

Mirams, L., Poliakoff, E., Brown, R.J. and Lloyd, D.M. (2012) 'Interoceptive and exteroceptive attention have opposite effects on subsequent somatosensory perceptual decision making.' *Quarterly Journal of Experimental Psychology 65*, 926–938.

Music, G. (2019) *Nurturing Children*. Abingdon: Routledge.

National Child Traumatic Stress Network (NCTSN) (n.d.) 'Complex trauma.' Accessed on 02/03/20 at www.nctsn.org/what-is-child-trauma/trauma-types/complex-trauma.

Pollatos, O., Kirsch, W. and Schandry, R. (2005) 'On the relationship between interoceptive awareness, emotional experience, and brain processes.' *Brain Research. Cognitive Brain Research 25*, 948–962.

Pollatos, O., Kurz, A.-L., Albrecht J., Schreder, T. *et al.* (2008) 'Reduced perception of bodily signals in anorexia nervosa.' *Eating Behaviors 9*, 381–388.

Porges, S. (1993) 'The infant's sixth sense: Awareness and regulation of bodily processes.' *Zero to Three 14*, 12–16.

Porges, S. (2017) *The Pocket Guide to the Polyvagal Theory*. New York, NY: W.W. Norton & Company.

Putnam, F.W. (1997) *Dissociation in Children and Adolescents: A Developmental Perspective*. New York, NY: The Guildford Press.

Saxe, G.N., Ellis, B.H. and Kaplow, J.B. (2007) *Collaborative Treatment and Traumatized Children and Teens*. New York, NY: Guildford Publications.

Schaefer, M., Egloff, B. and Witthöft, M. (2012) 'Is interoceptive awareness really altered in somatoform disorders? Testing competing theories with two paradigms of heartbeat perception.' *Journal of Abnormal Psychology 121*, 3, 719–724.

Schmidt, A.J., Gierlings, R.E. and Peters, M.L. (1989) 'Environmental and interoceptive influences on chronic low back pain behavior.' *Pain 38*, 137–143.

Schwartz, A. (2019) 'Complex PTSD and dissociative symptoms.' Accessed on 26/03/20 at https://drarielleschwartz.com/complex-ptsd-and-dissociative-symptoms-dr-arielle-schwartz/#.XvTEsyhKiUk.

Siegel, D.J. (2010) *Mindsight: The New Science of Personal Transformation.* New York, NY: Bantam Books.

Silberg, J. (2012) *The Child Survivor: Healing Developmental Trauma and Dissociation.* New York, NY: Routledge.

Van der Hart, O., Nijenhuis, E.R.S. and Steele, C. (2006) *The Haunted Self: Structural Dissociation and the Treatment of Chronic Traumatisation.* New York, NY: W.W. Norton & Company.

van der Kolk, B. (2014) *The Body Keeps the Score.* New York, NY: Penguin.

van der Kolk, B. (n.d.) 'Developmental Trauma Disorder.' Accessed on 26/03/20 at https://traumaticstressinstitute.org/wp-content/files_mf/1276541701VanderKolkDvptTraumaDis.pdf.

Waters, F. (2016) *Healing the Fractured Child.* New York, NY: Springer Publishing Company.

Watkins, J.G. and Watkins, H.H. (1979) 'The Theory and Practice of Egostate Therapy.' In H. Grayson (ed.) *Short Term Approaches to Psychotherapy.* New York, NY: Human Sciences Press.

Wieland, S. (2011) *Dissociation in Traumatised Children and Adolescents.* New York, NY: Routledge.

INDEX

Sub-headings in *italics* indicate figures.